AUSTRALIA'S
HISTORY

MARTYN LYONS is Professor of History and Associate Dean for Research in the Faculty of Arts and Social Sciences at the University of New South Wales. He has published widely on French revolutionary and Napoleonic history, and on the history of the book and reading practices in Europe and Australia.

PENNY RUSSELL lectures in Australian history, autobiography and scandal at the University of Sydney. She is the author of *A Wish of Distinction: Colonial Gentility and Femininity* and *This Errant Lady: Jane Franklin's Overland Journey to Port Phillip and Sydney 1839*.

AUSTRALIA'S
HISTORY
Themes and Debates

edited by
MARTYN LYONS and PENNY RUSSELL

A UNSW Press book

Published by
University of New South Wales Press Ltd
University of New South Wales
Sydney NSW 2052
AUSTRALIA
www.unswpress.com.au

National Library of Australia
Cataloguing-in-Publication entry

Lyons, Martyn, 1946– .
   Australia's history: themes and debates.
   Includes index.
   ISBN 0 86840 790 9.
   1. Australia - History. I. Russell, Penelope Ann.
   II. Title.

   994

Design Di Quick
Print Griffin Press
Cover image Donald Friend, *Bennelong's Duel with Colebee*, 1964.
Reproduced with permission from the Estate of the late Donald
Friend. Collection: Sydney Opera House Trust, bequest of Dr Stuart
Scougall, 1970.

CONTENTS

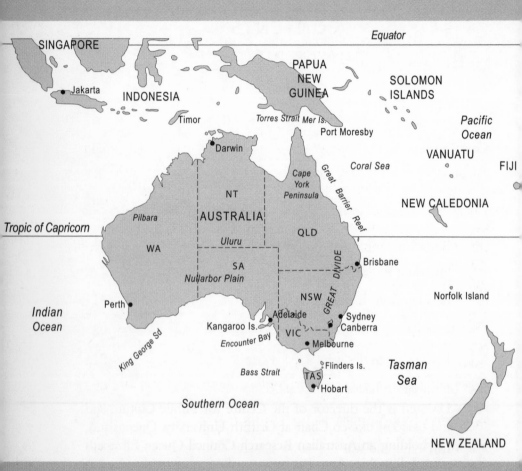

Australia and its region

CONTRIBUTORS

CATRIONA ELDER is a lecturer in the Department of Sociology and Social Policy at the University of Sydney. Her recent work has focused on issues of race relations in Australia in the twentieth century.

CHARLIE FOX teaches in the History Department at the University of Western Australia, Perth. His research interests include the history of the 1960s, work and unemployment. His latest book *Fighting Back: the politics of the unemployed in Victoria in the Great Depression*, was published in 2000.

REGINA GANTER is senior lecturer in the School of Arts, Media and Culture at Griffith University, Queensland. Her book *The Pearl-Shellers of Torres Strait* received the inaugural Australian history prize of the Australian Historical Association. Another book, *Mixed Relations: Asian/Aboriginal contact in north Australia*, is forthcoming in 2005.

ANNA HAEBICH is the director of the Centre for Public Culture and Ideas and ORBICOM UNESCO Chair at Griffith University, Queensland, as well as holding an Australian Research Council Queen Elizabeth II Research Fellowship. Anna has two award-winning publications in Indigenous Australian history: *Broken Circles* and *For Their Own Good*.

ALISON HOLLAND is a lecturer in the Department of Modern History at Macquarie University, Sydney. She is a contributor to Anna Cole et al (eds), *Uncommon Ground: white women in Aboriginal history*, and to Tim Rowse (ed), *Contesting Assimilation: histories of colonial and Indigenous initiatives* (both forthcoming).

MARTYN LYONS is professor of History and associate dean for Research in the Faculty of Arts and Social Sciences at the University of New South Wales. He has published widely on French revolutionary and Napoleonic history, and on the history of the book and reading practices in Europe and Australia.

SEAMUS O'HANLON teaches in the School of Historical Studies at Monash University in Melbourne. His recent books include *Together Apart: boarding house, hostel and flat life in pre-war Melbourne*, shortlisted for the New South Wales Premier's History Prize in 2003, and *GO!: Melbourne in the sixties*, co-edited with Tanja Luckins.

MELANIE OPPENHEIMER is senior lecturer in Australian history at the University of Western Sydney. She has written extensively on many aspects of volunteering from both an historical and contemporary perspective. Her books include *Volunteers and Volunteering* and *All Work No Pay: Australian civilian volunteers in war*.

PENNY RUSSELL lectures in Australian history, autobiography and scandal at the University of Sydney. She is the author of *A Wish of Distinction: colonial gentility and femininity*, and *This Errant Lady: Jane Franklin's overland journey to Port Phillip and Sydney 1839*.

BRUCE SCATES is associate professor in the School of History at the University of New South Wales. His major publications include *A New Australia: radicalism, citizenship and the First Republic* and (with Rae Frances) *Women and the Great War*.

DAVID WALKER is professor of Australian Studies at Deakin University, Victoria, and author of *Anxious Nation: Australia and the rise of Asia 1850 to 1939*, which won the Ernest Scott Prize for History in 2001.

RICHARD WHITE teaches in the Department of History, University of Sydney. His publications include *Inventing Australia* and, most recently, *Cultural History in Australia* (with Hsu-Ming Teo). His new book, *On Holidays: a history of getting away in Australia*, will be published in 2005.

TIMELINE

50 000 BCE	First traces of the presence of Indigenous Australians
1788	The 'First Fleet' of convicts arrived at Botany Bay
1803	Settlement of Van Diemen's Land (Tasmania)
1838	Myall Creek massacre (New South Wales), 28 Aborigines killed by convicts
1850	Britain passed Australian Colonies Government Act, leading to a measure of colonial self-government; gold discovered in New South Wales and Victoria
1852	Convict transportation to eastern Australia ended
1854	The 'Eureka Stockade' in Ballarat (Victoria), a gold miners' revolt inspired by vaguely republican ideologies, was supressed by troops
1856	South Australia first colony of the British Empire to introduce universal male suffrage; Lambing Flat (New South Wales) anti-Chinese riots and killings in the gold fields
1876	National trade unions legalised

1880	Execution of the bushranger Ned Kelly, a folk hero of Irish origin
1885	Establishment of 'Broken Hill Proprietary Limited' (BHP: a producer of coal, steel, minerals, manufactures)
1890	Collapse of the great strike of sailors and maritime industries
1891	Creation of the Australian Labor Party
1891 & 1894	Sheep-shearers' strikes defeated with non-unionised workers
1894	Women got the vote in South Australia; 16 500 Australians participated in the Boer War in South Africa
1901	Federation: the six colonies (New South Wales, Victoria, South Australia, Queensland, Tasmania, Western Australia) became the united federal 'Commonwealth of Australia'
1901	Beginning of the White Australia policy to limit Asian immigration
1902	*Commonwealth Franchise Act* gave women the right to vote in Australian federal elections
1904	The first federal Labor government another 'world first'
1904	The *Commonwealth Arbitration and Conciliation Act* inaugurated the Commonwealth Arbitration Court to judge industrial conflicts
1915	Allies attacked Turkey at Gallipoli; 9000 troops of the Australian and New Zealand Army Corps (ANZACs) killed
1916 & 1917	Two referenda on conscription produced victories for the 'No' vote, and split the Labor Party
1941	Prime Minister John Curtin declared Australia would 'look to America'

1942 Fall of Singapore: 18 000 Australian troops taken prisoner; Japanese later halted on Kokoda Track

1946 Beginning of Anglo-Australian nuclear testing at Maralinga (South Australia); *Nationality and Citizenship Act* created Australian citizenship, complementing existing 'British subject' status

1948-66 Liberal Party in government under Prime Minister Robert Menzies

1951 ANZUS Treaty (a security pact between Australia, New Zealand and the United States); proposal to abolish the Communist Party defeated at referendum

1955 Arrival of the one-millionth post-war immigrant

1963-72 50 000 Australians participated in Vietnam War

1963 Yirrkala Aborigines of North Queensland presented bark petition to Parliament requesting land rights

1964 First legal disputes between Aborigines and mining companies

1965 'Freedom ride', led by Aboriginal activist Charles Perkins, protest against racial discrimination

1967 Constitutional changes to give Aborigines full civil and political rights carried at referendum by a large majority

1970 100 000 participate in the 'Vietnam Moratorium' in Melbourne: the largest demonstration in Australian history

1972-75 Labor government under prime minister Gough Whitlam: the end of the White Australia policy, withdrawal of troops from Vietnam, independence for Papua New Guinea, recognition of the People's Republic of China

1972 Aboriginal Tent Embassy erected by Aboriginal protesters outside ('Old') Parliament House: remains a site for protest to this day

1975 *Racial Discrimination Act* outlawed discrimination on the basis of race

1987 Office of Multicultural Affairs established

1988 Australia celebrated its bicentennial of white settlement

1992 The Mabo judgment: in the case of *Mabo vs Queensland no 2*, the High Court (Australia's highest jurisdiction) inserted the doctrine of Aboriginal landownership ('native title') into common law, replacing the doctrine of *terra nullius* (territory without tenured occupation) on which British possession had been based

1996 The Wik judgment: the High Court ruled in the *Wik* case that a pastoral lease did not necessarily extinguish native title

1996 'Stolen Generations', the report of a human rights inquiry into the forced removal of Aboriginal children from their families for assimilation into white society, published

1999 Australia rejected republic in referendum

2000 Sydney hosted Olympic Games

2002 88 Australians die in a nightclub bombing in Bali, Indonesia

2003 Australian Defence Forces joined the 'Coalition of the Willing' in Iraq

INTRODUCTION

In the European imagination, Australia has for a long time seemed a place of fantasy, a land full of natural curiosities, a living museum of the bizarre and miraculous where the natural order is inverted. In 1864 Jules Verne described it as a world upside down:

> where every year the trees lose their bark instead of their leaves; where leaves present their profile to the sun and not their face, and where trees give no shade; ... where the kangaroo bounds along on uneven paws; where sheep have the heads of pigs; where foxes fly from tree to tree; where swans are black; where rats make nests ... ; a bizarre land if ever there was one, defying logic, a country of unnatural paradoxes! ... a sort of parody of universal laws, or rather a challenge to them thrust in the face of the rest of the world![1]

Seen through European eyes, Australia's originality was defined only by its departure from European norms. As the nineteenth century proceeded, the idea of Australia as a reverse utopia (sometimes a dystopia) also shaped the European vision of its social composition. In this land of opportunity the common man made a fortune and lorded it over those who were gentle by birth. In the words of one obscure novelist, 'This is the Anti-podes, you know. Everything is upside down.'[2] Such habits of speech tended to obscure the individuality of Australia's historical trajectory.

In the mid-nineteenth century, however, the six Australian colonies (New South Wales, Queensland, South Australia, Tasmania, Victoria and Western Australia) had obtained a certain degree of political autonomy. As the colonies moved towards independence, a more complex relationship between the metropolis and the periphery emerged. In 1901, another landmark was reached when the colonies 'federated', to become a single Australian Commonwealth, with Canberra – eventually – as the national capital. Then Australian troops, defending the solidarity of the British Empire, introduced Australia into the international arena, first in the Boer War (South African War) and then in World War I. The disastrous Gallipoli landing in the Dardanelles in 1915, where a quarter of allied casualties were Australian, became a powerful foundation myth for the Australian nation. According to one popular version of this myth, the virile heroism of the Australian soldier was betrayed by British arrogance and incompetence. Anzac Day (the acronym for the Australian and New Zealand Army Corps involved at Gallipoli), celebrated on 25 April, remains an important, if contested, national festival to the present day.

Like the armed forces of Anzac, Australian historiography was dominated by imperial influences during the first half of the twentieth century. The history of Britain, its empire and the evolution of its parliamentary constitution formed the basis of history taught in the school curriculum. Even when the historical discipline in Australia became more professionalised, it still remained profoundly influenced by the English training of its practitioners and by the context of the empire. Until 1927, no year-long university courses in Australian history were offered anywhere. Only in 1947 was the first doctorate awarded for work in the field of national history. By 1973, although Australian universities employed over 400 full-time historians, many of them had been recruited from Britain in the 1950s.[3]

In spite of this, the main questions which twentieth-century Australian historians were asking involved a search for a specific national identity. In this respect, the decade of the 1890s was once regarded as a formative period, in which a certain idea of Australianness

emerged. This sense of identity was rooted in a democratic egalitarianism, associated with the sheep-shearers and small farmers of rural
Australia. Pioneer values were stressed, along with the resourcefulness, determination and good humour of the bushman. These masculine virtues of the 'bush' and the outback, celebrated by novelists
and balladeers, came to be defined as specifically Australian. Australian radicalism was preferred to the politics of rich Anglophile settlers, and the 'natural' qualities of the bush seemed superior to the
more cosmopolitan sophistication of city life. This democratic
version of Australian nationalism in the late nineteenth century
inspired the first attempts to decolonise Australian history-writing.
The labour movement was one beneficiary of this development.
Reinforced, like the historiography of the labour movement itself, by
anti-British traditions derived from the descendants of Irish Catholic
immigrants, it developed an image of a radical, nationalist Australia.

   In the last 40 years, this orthodox view of Australian history has
more or less disintegrated. Two crucial events contributed to the rad-
icalisation of a whole generation of Australian historians. The first
was the opposition to the Vietnam War, in which 50 000 Australian
troops were engaged between 1965 and 1972. The second was the
political and constitutional crisis of 1975, when the Labor prime
minister, Gough Whitlam, was removed from office by the governor-
general (the representative of the British crown) even though his
government had a majority in the lower house. Whitlam, for many
an inspiring and imposing figure, led the first Labor government
since 1949. He had recalled Australian troops from Vietnam, and his
government represented hope for social change and for more positive relations with Asia.

   The Vietnam War and the dismissal of Whitlam took place within
a rapidly changing society. The acceleration of European immigration after World War II, the heightened anxieties of the Cold War,
and the impact of international civil rights movements shaped a generation of historians who were further radicalised by these internal
political controversies. They became in consequence more alert to

social issues, more aware of the subordination of Australia to Britain and later the United States, and more sensitive to the fate of ethnic minorities and other groups formerly excluded from Australian history-writing. Historiography became more open, more aware of divisions and conflicts in the national past, and more sceptical of consensual mythologies – like those which were trumpeted in 1988 during the commemoration of the bicentenary of white Australia.

Today the notion of progressive and egalitarian nationalism poses serious problems. In the late nineteenth century, it had racist and xenophobic overtones, just as expressions of European nationalisms did in the same era. As for the myth of the bush, there was always something paradoxical about the longing for a rural identity elaborated by one of the most urbanised societies on the planet. Furthermore, the nationalist myth – increasingly owned by the political right – was socially exclusive to a degree now considered by many to be inadmissible. It either obscured the Aboriginal presence, while denying the fact of black resistance to white colonisation, or else stifled it in paternalist condescension. And it was a specifically masculine myth, shaped by male values which left little space in the narrative for women. It became clear that there was a dimension missing from the history of Australian identity: the dimension of gender relations.

In building on this *prise de conscience*, Australian historiography has absorbed the intellectual currents and influences which have enriched the historical discipline worldwide. Feminist historiography, for example, has many notable representatives in the Australian scholarly community. They look to British and North American rather than to European models, but not slavishly so, since what applies in these contexts is not necessarily easily exportable to the Australian situation.[4] The 'linguistic turn' has helped to change the way Australian historiography analyses the discourses of race and gender difference.[5] The recent popularity of studies in history and memory also echoes international developments and often pays lip-service to the work of Pierre Nora.[6] These international influences provide ammunition for questioning and undermining the old certainties of progressive, nationalist historiography. They will be evident to any reader of the main journals publishing Australian history today: *Labour History*, published in Sydney, whose scope is much wider than its title suggests; and *Australian Historical Studies*, published in Melbourne. *History Australia*, the newly renovated journal of the Australian Historical Association, will further contribute to national history debates.

In connecting with international intellectual life, however, Australian history-writing does not simply mirror foreign fashions. It has some very distinctive problems and issues to confront, as the contributions to this volume are designed to demonstrate. Foremost among these is the Aboriginal question, which now comprises some highly politicised reflections on the whole process of colonisation, frontier violence and dispossession. Echoes of this debate are heard loud and clear in chapters by Anna Haebich and Alison Holland. The success of historians throughout the 1980s and 1990s in drawing attention to the destructive impact of colonisation has generated an increasingly virulent conservative backlash in the past decade. In 1993, distinguished historian Geoffrey Blainey drew up a 'balance sheet' of what had been good and bad in 'our history'. He coined the phrase 'black armband' history to designate the 'gloomy' view of the past, which he believed had come to dominate historical interpretation. He called for a more balanced judgment in which the 'lamentable' treatment of Aborigines was outweighed by the success story of colonisation. A few years later Keith Windschuttle went further, casting doubt on the story of dispossession itself and claiming that accounts of massacres of Aboriginal people had been 'fabricated' by Australian historians in the grip of an academic orthodoxy. The implications of this controversy spread far beyond the reach of academic history, and have been played out in a highly publicised, though highly simplified, media debate. The stakes are high, with the Right perceiving and seizing an opportunity to replace a politics of 'reconciliation' between black and white with a reassertion of the integrity of a proud and highly nationalist tradition.[7]

The anxiety surrounding national tradition in this debate reflects a second theme: the continued obsession with national identity and belonging. The obsession is perhaps unsurprising given Australia's history as a country of immigration, discussed in Catriona Elder's contribution. Founded on British and Irish immigration, white Australian society began to become much more socially and culturally diverse only with the post-World War II wave of migration from Greece, Italy and war-ravaged eastern Europe. Since then, large numbers of immigrants have settled in Australia from Asian countries, and even more recently from South Africa, the Middle East and the countries of the former Soviet Union.

This history and cultural diversity produces various reactions: on one hand, the insecurity and xenophobia which fuelled Pauline Hanson's One Nation Party; on the other, official government recognition since the 1980s of the needs of a pluralistic society. The idea of 'multiculturalism' in this sense enjoys widespread (but not unchallenged) support in Australia, and it is important to distinguish it from European interpretations of the concept. Whereas in some European contexts multiculturalism signifies a threat to social cohesion, and seems to herald the emergence of divisive, community-based identity politics, in Australia the term encourages respect for cultural difference and a recognition of Australia's distinctive path of social development. The uncertainties of an immigrant society have fed a continual quest for the foundations of national distinctiveness, seen equally in the preoccupation with manners of nineteenth-century society discussed by Penny Russell, or the complex history of national symbols analysed by Richard White. It is often argued that the same uncertainty has underpinned Australia's enthusiastic involvement in imperial and foreign wars, though Melanie Oppenheimer and Bruce Scates offer a broader discussion of the social impact of those wars in this volume.

Thirdly, the perennial question of reconciling Australia's history with its geography remains unresolved. Australia has historically been a highly urbanised society, although its economy has depended upon the rural industries of pastoralism and mining as much as its cultural nationalism has drawn from the powerful mythology of the bush. In his discussion of aspects of Australian urban history, Seamus O'Hanlon reassesses Australian suburbia, which has at various moments embodied the dreams of a home-owning society and the nightmare of stultifying social and cultural conformity. Australia's unique position as a former British settler colony perched on the edge of Asia produces another permanent dilemma, which is reflected in several chapters in this book. The contributions of David Walker, Regina Ganter and Charlie Fox all touch in different ways on Australia's relationship both now and historically with Asia. Ganter and Fox in particular also draw attention to the dangers of generalising national experience across a vast continent, where regional diversity is often more significant than the cultural or political homogeneity imagined at its centre.

>─┤◆>─◎─<◆├─<

The idea for this volume came from Robin Derricourt, managing director of UNSW Press. It is produced to coincide with the twentieth International Congress of the Historical Sciences (CISH), convened at UNSW in Sydney in July 2005. The project was enthusiastically endorsed by the Australian Historical Association and the CISH Congress Organising Committee, and contributions were 'workshopped' at the association's 2004 conference in Newcastle, New South Wales. Inevitably, some important areas have not been covered in our collection, including labour history and the history of the environment. As editors, however, we have not aimed at a comprehensive coverage of Australian history, which would have been impossible in such a short volume. Instead, we commissioned a selection of contributors who were invited to assess the state of research in their area of current involvement. The topics presented are therefore all 'live' topics, and many are handled by younger scholars at the forefront of work in their respective fields. We have tried to dilute the usual preponderance of Sydney and Melbourne by including contributors based elsewhere, and by looking north and west for fresh subject-matter. We have aimed throughout to illuminate the contemporary concerns of Australian historians for an audience of interested non-specialists in the field, the majority of whom may have little previous knowledge of Australia's rich history. We would like to acknowledge the support of the Australian Historical Association's executive committee and of UNSW Press in launching the project.

Martyn Lyons, UNSW
Penny Russell, University of Sydney

Notes

1   Jules Verne, *Les Enfants du Capitaine Grant*, Paris, 1982, vol 1, p 412 (this trans. by M Lyons).
2   Elizabeth Murray, *Ella Norman, or, A Woman's Perils*, Melbourne, 1985 (first published 1864), p 39.
3   Stuart Macintyre, 'The writing of Australian history', in D H Borchardt (ed), *Australians: a guide to sources*, Sydney, 1987, p 22.
4   For example Marilyn Lake, *Getting Equal: the history of Australian feminism*, Sydney, 1999; Susan Magarey et al (eds), *Debutante Nation: feminism contests the 1890s*, Sydney, 1993; and Patricia Grimshaw et al, *Creating a Nation*, Melbourne, 1994.
5   For example Paul Carter, *The Road to Botany Bay*, London, 1987; or Jennifer Rutherford, *The Gauche Intruder*, Melbourne, 2000.
6   Paula Hamilton and Kate Darian-Smith (eds), *Memory and History in Twentieth-Century Australia*, Melbourne, 1994.
7   See S Macintyre and A Clark, *The History Wars*, Melbourne, 2003, especially chs 7 and 8; Keith Windschuttle, *The Fabrication of Aboriginal History, volume 1: Van Diemen's Land 1803-1847*, Sydney, 2002.

CHAPTER ONE

THE BATTLEFIELDS
OF ABORIGINAL HISTORY

ANNA HAEBICH

Aboriginal history is the battleground of Australian history. Over the past three decades, its proponents have fought to replace national myths of benign settlement and unimpeded progress with discomforting histories of colonial invasion and destruction driven by demand for land and resources at any cost. These counter-histories have played a central role in national debates over native title, sovereignty, Aboriginal deaths in custody, Mabo, the 'Stolen Generations' and more recently stolen wages – debates that have prompted a crisis in national conscience and identity. The heated exchanges in Australia's 'History Wars' are proof of the high stakes involved. As historian Mark McKenna noted recently, the repercussions are 'testament to the power of history to alter the political and social landscape in which we live'.[1] This chapter outlines the contested beginnings, voices and truths of these histories of Aboriginal/white relations, and introduces recent controversies over Australia's frontier history and the Stolen Generations.

Contested beginnings

The academic study of Aboriginal history has two legendary foundational moments, neither involving professional historians. The first was in 1969 when anthropologist WEH Stanner, delivering the Boyer Lectures to a national radio audience, called for an end to the 'great Australian silence' about the history of the 'unacknowledged relations between two racial groups' within the nation. The next moment came in 1970 with the publication of the groundbreaking three-volume history of Aboriginal oppression and institutionalised racism, *Aboriginal Policy and Practice*, by social scientist and bureaucrat Charles D Rowley. This provided the blue-print for the new historical consciousness demanded by Stanner.[2]

Ironically, the 'great Australian silence' that Rowley and Stanner addressed was largely a phenomenon of twentieth-century academic history. Early colonists left a lively archive of accounts of both amicable and violent encounters, exploitative and humanitarian relations, and public debates about Aborigines' fate in newspapers, personal memoirs and professional histories. However, for much of the twentieth century, historians ignored this entwined past in favour of histories of nation and nation-building. These recounted a heroic colonial past and mapped a noble future, and indelibly stamped white ownership and supremacy across the continent. They presented a vision of a united and uniform White Australia where whiteness bestowed citizenship, status, power and privilege. Historian Walter Murdoch voiced the general disdain when he gave his reason for excluding Aborigines from his popular school text *Making of Australia: an introductory history* (1917):

> When people talk about 'the history of Australia' they mean the history of the white people who have lived in Australia … We should not stretch the term to make it include the history of the dark skinned wandering tribes … for they have nothing that can be called history.[3]

Such views were a product of entrenched racist attitudes that framed the notorious White Australia policy and discriminatory legislation adopted by federal and state governments at the time of Federation in 1901. Aboriginal people's lives were controlled and regulated, and they were excluded from processes of nation and the rights and benefits bestowed by citizenship. Rendered invisible through segregation in isolated institutions, reserves and rigid 'caste' barriers, they slipped from the social landscape and from the nation's official history.

Stanner acknowledged that in mid-twentieth-century Australia there was no blanket, nation-wide silence 'on all matters aboriginal'; rather there was 'a real and growing appreciation of the distinctive quality of aboriginal culture, thought, and problems of life'.[4] Outside the halls of academic history, there was an outpouring of stories about the Aboriginal past and present, accompanied by a rising chorus of Aboriginal voices recounting their own versions of the past.

At the time of first European contact in the eighteenth century, rich and diverse Aboriginal cultures flourished across the continent. There were perhaps as many as 600 distinct languages, along with diverse lifestyles based on detailed traditional environmental knowledges, and complex kinship, religious and ceremonial practices and beliefs whose origins stretched back across the millennia into the 'Dreaming'. Aboriginal curator Djon Mundine describes the Dreaming as 'the reality of the spirit worlds. It exists at the beginning of time, into the present and continues into the future.'[5] This body of mythic origins and traditions was recounted, performed and committed to memory through rigorous training over lifetimes. In post-contact times, Aboriginal nations also committed to memory their own narratives of colonial history, employing traditional forms of oration, performance and visual representation, the conventions of which contrasted markedly with methods of Western history. Largely isolated within Aboriginal worlds, these histories and traditions, as interpreted by anthropologists and white artists, attracted considerable public interest in Australia during the 1950s and 1960s.

Academic historians may have left Aboriginal history out of their narratives of nation, but explanations of this past continued to circulate within the public domain. These accounts shaped popular understanding about the Aboriginal past, present and future from the late nineteenth century into the 1970s, and represent a significant and hitherto neglected aspect of Australia's past. Produced largely by white male observers – missionaries, government officials, employers, travellers, anthropologists and artists – these accounts appeared in mission tracts, government reports, personal memoirs, press articles, travel books, films, exhibitions, art and literature. As Aboriginal academic Marcia Langton has observed, these 'stories told by former colonists' had a particular power in a racially segregated society where contact between black and white was limited.[6] The level of shared theoretical, factual and stylistic features masked subjective frameworks and agendas, and created a mutually reinforcing circuitry of information that was accepted as factual and that went largely unchallenged. These accounts also influenced larger conceptual frameworks and categories that made possible or constrained policy and practice in relation to Aboriginal people. They were also the source of information, imagery, motifs and themes for representations in museums, literary, artistic and other cultural productions, and in domestic settings. Importantly, and despite their faults, they filled in the gaps about the Aboriginal past in Australia's national histories.

The two paradigms of 'social evolution' and 'assimilation' permeated these understandings. These global paradigms were based on the premise of the ultimate disappearance of indigenous peoples, whether by physical extinction or through merging into the dominant society. Social evolution ruled from the late nineteenth century to the 1930s, while assimilation was official government policy from the 1950s until the 1970s, when it was abandoned for more progressive policies. In practice, the paradigms operated coterminously. Aboriginal anthropologist Ian Anderson argues there was no 'radical historical juncture' only shifts in emphasis – social evolution and assimilation were 'flip sides of the same coin'.[7] Both continued to influence public imaginings of the past long after they were officially abandoned. In the Australian context they were shaped by anthropological theory and research. Their nexus with official policies and practice meant that the trajectories they predicted for Aboriginal populations became reflected in lived outcomes.

Social evolution provided an explanation for the tragic and fatal impact of Western colonialism around the world. Based on Social Darwinism and promoted as scientific fact, it was a circular, imaginary proposition based on ethnological fragments collected by amateurs in the field and cobbled together by armchair anthropologists in distant Europe into vast evolutionary histories of mankind. Indigenous societies were positioned at the bottom rung of the evolutionary ladder as relics of a distant Stone Age past. In the clash between 'primitive' and 'civilised', they were 'doomed to extinction'. Since the laws of nature ordained their demise, colonists were absolved from acting to halt Indigenous deaths. This provided the rationale for policies of protection and practices of enforced segregation in isolated reserves where Aborigines could be sheltered from the onslaught of civilisation while they quietly passed away. Meanwhile unchecked expansion into their lands continued, along with forced labour and sexual exploitation. This paradigm also influenced turn-of-the-century cultural representations. While Aboriginal people became a passing footnote in national histories, in literature and the visual arts they provided a powerful symbol of a passing natural world and a poignant though affirming backdrop to the progress of white Australia. These representations maintained a powerful hold on the Australian imagination, long after the public panics about Aboriginal population recovery in the 1930s and the abandonment of evolutionary theory by anthropologists. Marcia Langton claims that to this day many non-Indigenous Australians still cling to the 'trope of a "Stone Age" Aboriginal culture frozen in time' and of a 'limited, inflexible, utilitarian, animist and above all primitive way of life inexorably doomed to extinction'.[8]

Assimilation promised to remove even the passing historical footnote by erasing the Aboriginal past, present and future. From first contact, colonists envisaged a circumscribed form of assimilation with Aborigines kept as menial workers within the confines of colonial society but otherwise denied rights. State and later federal governments adopted legislation to enforce this from the late nineteenth century until the mid-twentieth. For the many Aborigines caught up in this web, life became a trajectory of forced removal from their families to the drudgery of institutions where they were trained for a life of servitude as labourers and domestic servants until finally, after years of back-breaking work, they finished up with no family, no savings and nowhere to go. This was particularly so for the many children of mixed descent who made up the Stolen Generations. In the 1930s in the Northern Territory and Western Australia, an extreme form of assimilation was adopted to progressively 'breed out' Aboriginal physical as well as cultural characteristics through forced state marriages between lighter castes and whites. A new positive version based on Aboriginal citizenship and equality, adopted in the early 1950s, promoted a vision of a culturally and racially harmonious nation drawing Aboriginal people, white settlers and migrants together as one. The discrediting of scientific racism and new explanations attributing disadvantage to social rather than racial factors paved the way for more optimistic programs of change based on the amelioration of social conditions and the promise of equality for all.

At this time anthropologists working with government dominated public knowledge about Aborigines. Anthropologist AP Elkin developed the model of assimilation which was then fine-tuned by the minister for Territories, Paul Hasluck (a former journalist who wrote the first history of Aboriginal administration in Western Australia in 1938). This policy stated that Aboriginal people were to become 'members of a single Australian community enjoying the same rights and privileges, accepting the same responsibilities, observing the same customs and influenced by the same beliefs, hopes and loyalties as other Australians'.[9]

Governments set out to repeal race-based discriminatory legislative and administrative frameworks, empty their institutions and give Aboriginal people access to all the services and benefits already available to other Australians. Although structural goals were achieved, institutionalised racism continued and there was a new focus on cultural essentialism as government officers and anthropologists monitored the progress of 'detribalised' people towards assimilated life across several 'dichotomised barriers': 'black culture into white culture; out of tradition into white history; from the camp into town; swapping a black skin for a white one'.[10]

Elkin also provided a model of historical change to replace earlier evolutionary stages. This proposed a series of culturally determined phases that moved inexorably from 'tentative approach', 'clash', 'intelligent parasitism', 'intelligent appreciation' on both sides and eventually to Aboriginal assimilation and citizenship. This model shaped the brief histories written by anthropologists to introduce their studies of assimilation in southern Australian, such as Ronald and Catherine Berndt's study of South Australian Aborigines, which combined the insights of anthropological fieldwork with limited archival research.[11]

Ironically, this desire for seamless assimilation coincided with a burst of public interest in unassimilated Aborigines' cultural forms and ponderings about their experiences along the road to assimilation. Federal and state governments produced pamphlets, films, lectures and press reports explaining and promoting assimilation to audiences in Australia and overseas. Prominent white Australian artists and writers – Arthur Boyd, Russell Drysdale, Beth Dean, Charles and Elsa Chauvel, Nene Gare – wedded Aboriginal cultural forms to the international aesthetics of Modernism in their search for symbols of national identity and works exploring the 'plight of the Aborigines'. Designers were similarly inspired by Aboriginal motifs popularised in publications by museum anthropologists Charles Mountford and Fred McCarthy. These developments were avidly reported in the popular press and magazines such as *Pix* and *Australia Post*, albeit expressed within the patronising terms of the paradigms of assimilation and social evolution.

A clamour of interest, rather than a deep silence, provided the context for the emergence of academic Aboriginal history. The fresh insights into Aboriginal culture and the past that this produced challenged existing paradigms and assumptions, and created a need for new ways to reinterpret history. The methodologies of academic history promised one way of breaking away from these paradigms and of generating new narratives and perspectives to uncover the truth about Australia's entwined past.

The seismic shift in Australian history from the 1970s also reflected a further influence from outside the academy – the voices of Aboriginal protest that burst into the public domain during the 1960s and introduced white audiences to Aboriginal accounts of the past.[12] This also disrupted white domination of public discourse about Aborigines. Careful reading of press accounts of individual lives of prominent Aborigines – such as artist Albert Namatjira, opera singer Harold Blair, boxing champion Lionel Rose and political activist Kath Walker – provided insights into personal and family histories of poverty and oppression. The media introduced the young leader Charles Perkins, who led the 1965 American Civil Rights-inspired 'freedom rides' through rural New South Wales; and the distant community of Yirrkala, whose elders presented a bark petition to Federal Parliament in 1963 seeking return of control over their traditional lands. There were also the triumphant victories of the 1967 referendum to remove discriminatory clauses from the Australian Constitution; the 1968 granting of award wages to pastoral workers; the 1972 Aboriginal Tent Embassy in Canberra; and the 1976 *Northern Territory Land Rights Act*. Parallelling this public political voice was an emerging Aboriginal literary and artistic movement which informed enthusiastic audiences in Australia and overseas through words and images of the histories of Aboriginal families and communities.

Revisionist historians writing of the 1970s have not always acknowledged these influences; instead they identify international civil rights, anti-apartheid and anti-war movements as motivating factors. An exception is historian Henry Reynolds who told how his involvement with Aboriginal politics in north Queensland forced the realisation that:

to understand the contemporary situation it would be necessary to learn something about the history ... So that's where it began, in an attempt to understand both the contemporary situation, the situation in the past, and also to understand something about the way in which European history had been written in Australia.[13]

International social movements formed around gender, race, class and ethnicity were also generating new knowledges and methodologies within the discipline of history. In particular, social history provided new approaches for doing 'history from below' based on oral accounts of the everyday lives of ordinary people. There were other untapped sources for research – images, ethnographies, previously neglected archives and quantitative data – and new questions, theories, frameworks and collaborative ways of working with Aboriginal people. From this came a heady mix of studies of frontiers, administrations, legislation, institutions, labour and gender relations, communities, families and regions that were enthusiastically taken up by publishers catering for an eager public readership.

Contested voices

By the 1980s, this vanguard had successfully challenged the old national histories within the academy. They had also colonised the space previously dominated by anthropologists representing the Aboriginal past to white audiences. Their position became increasingly politicised, as they were drawn into national debates and their new roles were often discomforting. Aboriginal history proved a battle zone of unresolved tensions and disputes. During the 1980s, a strong Aboriginal lobby challenged historians' sole right to speak, and questioned the use of Western history to represent their past. Anthropologists and cultural studies theorists called on historians to critically assess their own methodologies, and to acknowledge the 'convergences between the narrative of Progress, the imperative to colonize, and history's disciplinary practices'.[14] However, the most heated battles began when the new histories began to seriously challenge parameters of conventional history in the public domain, prompting accusations that historians had abandoned scholarship to promote political agendas. These attacks attracted unprecedented media attention, but the issues between historians and Aboriginal people were far more complex and difficult to resolve.

Aboriginal challenges were motivated in part by dissatisfaction with the authorised bicentennial Australian history of 1988 – a view succinctly expressed by a group who threw copies into Sydney Harbour at the official launch by Prime Minister Bob Hawke. Having created a strong voice in the public domain, they were loath to share the 'precious resource' of their history with white historians.[15] They also pointed to contrasting Indigenous and Western historical conventions – oral versus written traditions, mythical pasts versus historical chronology and periodisation, ritual versus secular ownership of knowledge, mythical versus rationalist narrative structures, visual versus literary representation – and to incompatible values and divergent historical experiences.[16] They questioned how white historians could escape the rationales, narratives and tropes of colonialism embedded in their language and histories. In public lecture halls around the nation, they demanded that historians vacate the stage and leave Aboriginal people to speak in their own way and on their own terms. They also negotiated protocols for researchers, and agreements over control and access to historical records and objects, and the return of research findings and repatriation of human remains and artefacts to communities.

Despite these early attempts to gain the historical high ground, relatively few Aboriginal historians progressed to academic prominence over the years – notable exceptions being Jackie Huggins, Tony Birch, Jennifer Sabione, John Maynard, Barbara Cummings and curator Heather Sculthorpe. The major public sites have been in literature and the visual and performing arts: in the works of writers Jack Davis, Sally Morgan, Stephen Kinnane, Ruth Hegarty and Ruby Langford, Aboriginal artists including Fiona Foley, Leah King and Julie Dowling, and Bangarra Dance Theatre. Aboriginal leaders have created histories in other arenas through participation in government inquiries and public debates. Notable here are Pat Dodson's *Report on Underlying Issues in Western Australia* for the Royal Commission into Aboriginal Deaths in Custody (RCIADIC) and contributions to the Council for Aboriginal Reconciliation; and Mick Dodson's role as social justice commissioner for the 1996 Human Rights Equal Opportunity Commission's *Inquiry into Separation of Aboriginal and Torres Strait Islander Children from their Families* (HREOC Inquiry).

Some white historians have continued to write Aboriginal history within the academy isolated from Aboriginal communities or have shifted to related fields such as post-colonial or whiteness studies. Others have negotiated collaborative projects guided by Aboriginal community goals. They have also contributed to government inquiries and Royal Commissions. For example, those working for the RCIADIC collaborated on a national history of Aboriginal administrations edited by Ann McGrath, and Queensland historian Ros Kidd contributed to the *Cape York Justice Study*. They have collaborated in native title claims for regional land and seas councils, mining companies and the Native Title Tribunal, and have been called as expert court witnesses – prompting a lively debate about the differing nature of legal and historical evidence.[17] Others have worked closely with communities on regional histories. Carolyn Wadley Dowley wrote of her initial qualms about recording the history of the Wongutha people from Leonora, north of Kalgoorlie, in her book *Through Silent Country*:

> Previously I had been unsure as to whether I could, as a non-Aboriginal person, attempt to research and write about Aboriginal experience of Western Australian history. It was a complex ethical and moral issue … My problem was resolved by the people.[18]

Mary-Anne Jebb's entwined history of pastoral workers and white bosses in the north-east Kimberley combines archival sources with living memories collected through collaborative research over several years residence in the region. Mark McKenna's 'personal quest' to understand the history of his block of land in south-eastern New South Wales began in the archives but led him on a similar journey of research through place and memory with local Aboriginal people. At an institutional level, the Cultural Heritage Division of the NSW National Parks and Wildlife Service (now in the Department of Environment and Conservation) is also contributing to a growing appreciation of shared cultural attachments.[19]

Debate on this issue remains open. Historian Stuart Macintyre criticises 'claims for exclusive ownership of the past' and quotes Eric Hobsbawn's statement that it is the historian's duty 'to stand aside from the passion of identity politics'. He suggests instead that being open to the ideas and criticisms of others builds influence and authority for minority voices and their histories. By contrast anthropologist Patrick Wolfe argues forcefully that:

> The question of who speaks goes far beyond liberal concerns with equity, dialogue or access to the academy. Claims to authority over Indigenous discourse made from within the settler-colonial academy necessarily participate in the continuing usurpation of Indigenous space (invasion is a structure not an event).[20]

Contested truths

The History Wars is the title of Stuart Macintyre's and Anna Clark's study of recent public controversies and allegations of dishonest scholarship surrounding the rewriting of Australia's past.[21] The title is a reference to the heat of the battles and a link to similar contests in North America and Europe. Macintyre traces public anxiety back to the writings of eminent historian Manning Clark, whose break with celebratory historical traditions in the 1960s was considered by his critics a 'bitter and cynical' act, seething with hatred of Australia – despite claims in Clark's 1976 Boyer Lectures that he was simply telling the story of 'what had happened when a great civilisation was transplanted to our ancient land'. A further challenge was the repeal in the early 1970s of the policy of assimilation by the federal administration headed by HC Coombs and the adoption of the policy of self-determination, land rights and acknowledgment of past wrongs. In 1988 critics condemned the authorised bicentennial history for 'slighting the core values and sources of pride of most Australians' by emphasising past discriminatory treatment of women and Aboriginal people.[22] The actions of Labor Prime Minister Paul Keating in the early 1990s fuelled further anxieties. With speechwriter and historian Don Watson, Keating embarked on a project to build a proud 'Big Picture' history of national triumph, tolerance and egalitarianism that also acknowledged past injustices. In his Redfern speech in 1992, Keating forcefully reminded white Australians that:

> it was we who did the dispossessing. We took the traditional land and smashed the traditional way of life. We brought the disasters. The alcohol. We committed the murders. We took the children from their mothers. We practised discrimination and exclusion.[23]

This admission from the nation's leader prompted a backlash from nervous vested interests. In the following year historian Geoffrey Blainey coined his epithet 'black armband history' to encapsulate what he and many other Australians considered to be the 'excessive emphasis ... on past wrongs'.[24]

The murmuring of conservative revisionists grew loud with the election of John Howard as Liberal prime minister in 1996. Howard endorsed the 'Blainey view' – he praised the nation's record of 'heroic achievement', denied responsibility for past wrongs, and advised Australians to judge their forebears in the context of their times. Decrying what he called 'historical correctness', he called on historians to present the facts in a balanced manner. These criticisms fitted with his new policy of 'practical reconciliation' – a revitalised form of assimilation that would remove all special Aboriginal rights and services. Revisionists were appointed to governing bodies of major cultural institutions presenting history to the public, such as the Australian Broadcasting Corporation and the National Museum. *Quadrant* magazine provided a forum for their uncompromising attacks on the High Court's 'Mabo' judgment, frontier history, the Stolen Generations and on historians for creating a poisonous atmosphere of guilt and political correctness.

Contested frontiers

This was the context of the fierce debates that erupted over the nature of relations along Australia's colonial frontiers. In the first volume of his 1970 trilogy, *Destruction of Aboriginal Society*, Charles Rowley provided a model of frontier relations that challenged conventional accounts of peaceful settlement, and shaped subsequent frontier studies by Henry Reynolds and other 1970s revisionists. Historians Bain Attwood and Stephen Foster summarised this model as follows:

> Aborigines and Europeans used the land in quite incompatible ways as pastoralists' cattle and sheep ate, trampled and fouled Aborigines' sources of food and water; Aborigines were forced to steal the newcomers' stock and other property in order to survive and often launched attacks on the colonists; pastoralists and their men wreaked violence on Aborigines, killing large numbers in the course of conflict across the country.[25]

Points of discussion in public debate included levels of violence, estimates of injury and deaths on both sides, explanations for the dramatic decrease in Aboriginal populations from an estimated 750 000 in 1788 to only 60 000 by the 1920s, and the roles of the Native Police and humanitarian interventions.[26] By the end of the 1970s, Rowley's generalised model was being reassessed in regional studies that emphasised diversity created by variations in local terrain, climate, population densities and economic frontiers – pastoral, marine, mining or farming. A further shift came with the insertion of Aboriginal perspectives and agency in Henry Reynolds' seminal book, *The Other Side of the Frontier*.[27] Drawing on linguistic, archaeological, anthropological and historical methodologies to interpret an extensive range of colonial sources, Reynolds explored how Aboriginal cultural frameworks determined interactions along the frontier. This opened up a new field of inquiry that drew attention to the complexity of Aboriginal agency and to the diversity of Aboriginal responses from violent resistance to accommodation and co-operation in work – as explored in Reynolds' *With the White People* and Ann McGrath's study of the pastoral frontier as 'a site of intimacy'.[28] Later in the 1980s, historians' focus shifted to post-frontier studies of official policy, legislation, administration and governance of Aboriginal people, initially under the control of Colonial Office in London and then devolving to new states and Federal governments, as outlined in studies by Heather Goodall, Ros Kidd and Anna Haebich.[29]

In the mid-1990s these frontier histories came under attack. In 1994, Rod Moran, a journalist with the *West Australian* newspaper, claimed that the Forrest River Massacre of 1926 had never happened.[30] In 2000, Keith Windschuttle alleged in a three-part series in *Quadrant* entitled 'The myths of frontier massacres in Australian history' that the historical evidence was 'highly suspect' and that most accounts were 'very poorly founded, other parts [were] seriously mistaken and some of it [was] outright fabrication'; estimates of the death toll, notably Reynolds' estimate of 20 000 Aboriginal dead, were fanciful at best.[31] In the following year Windschuttle shifted his sights to the 'Contested Frontiers' display in the recently opened National Museum, which he claimed included factual errors and the 'complete fabrication' of a massacre at Bells Falls Gorge. (Subsequent checks by museum staff led to the removal of only two offending words from the interpretive panel text.) He also published his revisionist history of the Tasmanian frontier, *The Fabrication of History*. In December 2001, the National Museum hosted two days of debate with invited curators and historians, including Windschuttle, which ended in a stalemate and a collection of papers – *Frontier Conflict: the Australian experience*.[32] Meanwhile the Federal government ordered a review of the National Museum and at the end of 2003 replaced its director, the Indigenous bureaucrat Dawn Casey.

Aboriginal involvement in this debate was limited. Privately there was widespread opinion that this was 'whitefellas' quibbling about events that Aboriginal people knew had happened, and that taking part would be too frustrating and painful. Aboriginal leader Clynton Wanganeen did comment in the *Adelaide Advertiser* in 2002:

> The problem with Mr Windschuttle, revisionist historian [is] if it is not on a file, noted in a report or printed in a newspaper then it didn't happen … We have an oral history spanning thousands of years … Our stories talk about massacres, death, cruelty, racism and resistance. But Mr Windschuttle will have none of this.[33]

At the same time Aboriginal artists in the West Kimberley held an exhibition called 'Blood on the Spinifex' in which they told stories through paintings of their families' experiences of massacres within living memory in response to revisionist denials of a massacre at nearby Mistake Creek in 1915.[34]

Contested lives

The Stolen Generations was also a site of fierce debate in the late 1990s. The findings and recommendations of the 1996 HREOC Inquiry and the spectacular failure of litigation seeking compensation for victims of removal policies aroused unprecedented public interest. The inquiry's *Bringing Them Home Report* hit the best-seller lists, with 1300 related press reports in the month following its publication. The report documented the systematic forced removal of children mainly of mixed descent from their families by governments across Australia from the late nineteenth century to the 1960s. It estimated that between one and three out of every ten children were removed. Drawing on hundreds of hours of mainly Aboriginal testimony, *Bringing Them Home* described the children's dismal experiences in institutions, foster homes and adoptive families, and in forced employment in the community. It also documented the enduring legacy of these experiences. The report concluded that the removals constituted cultural genocide under United Nations' conventions, and were in breach of international law. At the least the government should make a formal national apology and provide financial compensation and special services, including counselling and family reunions, for victims and their families.

Historians played a significant role in this sensitive issue. Historian Peter Read first wrote about the Stolen Generations of New South Wales in 1981, and helped establish LinkUp to arrange family reunions. He has been a regular expert court witness, notably in the sensational murder trial of James Savage in the United States in 1989.[35] Aboriginal historian Barbara Cummings was a driving force in the Bringing Them Home Conference in Darwin in 1996 that triggered both the Kruger case in the High Court of Australia and the Cubillo-Gunner case in the Northern Territory Supreme Court. Also in 1996, Aboriginal historian Jackie Huggins sat as commissioner for the HREOC's hearings in Brisbane. In 2000, Anna Haebich published *Broken Circles*, the first national history of the Stolen Generations. The book begins with the tragic story of a young man Louis Johnson, born in Alice Springs and then taken to live in Perth by his loving adoptive parents, and whose racially motivated murder in 1992 shocked West Australians and motivated his family to support research into the issue. In 2003 Doreen Mellor and Anna Haebich co-edited the National Library publication *Many Voices*, a collection of papers based on hundreds of hours of interviews both with Aboriginal people removed from their families, and with administrators and carers.[36]

This exposure of systematic fragmenting of Aboriginal families was further shocking evidence of past wrongs and led to an outpouring of grief and sympathy as well as denial, anger and resentment by Australians from all walks of life. The Howard government's

response was to reject the inquiry's core findings and recommendations, and to divert public attention from the deeper issues. The minister for Aboriginal Affairs, John Herron, even denied semantically
there had been a 'generation' stolen. This laid the basis for a 'culture
of denial and recrimination' that disfigured public debate over this
highly emotive issue and allowed the truth to be 'all but lost in a
cloud of polemic'.[37]

Once again *Quadrant* provided a forum for conservative critics
who questioned the report's reliance on unsubstantiated oral testimony, its inflated estimate of child removals, and the charge of cultural genocide – which they claimed had no legal standing under the
1948 UN Genocide Convention. They alleged that the children had
been rescued from physical and moral danger, and that their treatment was humane when judged by standards of the times. Further
doubts were raised by the conclusion of the Northern Territory
Supreme Court in 2000 that lead plaintiffs in the Cubillo-Gunner
case had subconsciously engaged in 'reconstruction, based, not on
what they knew at the time, but on what they have convinced themselves must have happened or what others may have told them'.[38]

In the same year, ignoring the recommendations of *Bringing
Them Home Report*, the prime minister issued a compromise 'statement of regret' and released funding of $63 million for government
departments to address 'family separation and its consequences'.
Political analyst Robert Manne critically addressed the government's
position and the many attacks on the report in his essay *In Denial*,[39]
and historian Bain Attwood broached issues of memory and history
in his discussion of the 'stolen generations narrative'.[40] However,
scepticism about the report and the so-called 'myth of the stolen generations' had taken hold, and it was not long before the public relegated the issue to the 'too hard' basket and the media allowed it to
slip quietly from its agenda.

At present (2004), an uneasy quiet pervades the battlefields of
Aboriginal history. While debate continues within academic circles,
media and public attention has shifted to issues of international ter-

rorism and refugees. Even the gross injustices exposed by current research into 'stolen wages' – governments' mishandling of controlled private savings and trust funds collected from Aborigines' wages, deceased estates and benefits – have failed to attract attention. The Howard government has quietly pursued its agenda of 'practical reconciliation', disbanding the nationally elected Aboriginal and Torres Strait Islander Commission and transferring Aboriginal-controlled services to mainstream government departments with few protests from the Australian public. The confronting issues raised by Aboriginal history have been left largely unresolved, and remain like open wounds. It is not yet time to bury the dead and send the troops home.

Notes

1   Mark McKenna, *Looking for Blackfellas' Point: an Australian history of place*, Sydney, 2002, p 7.
2   WEH Stanner, *After the Dreaming: black and white Australians – an anthropologist's view*, Sydney, 1969, pp 18 and 25; CD Rowley, *The Destruction of Aboriginal Society: outcasts in white Australia*, and *The Remote Aborigines*, Melbourne, 1972.
3   Cited in Ann Curthoys, 'Constructing national histories', in Bain Attwood and SG Foster (eds), *Frontier Conflict: the Australian experience*, Canberra, 2003, p 193.
4   Stanner, *After the Dreaming*, p 53.
5   Cited in Larissa Behrendt, *Achieving Social Justice: Indigenous rights and Australia's future*, Sydney, 2003, p 33.
6   Marcia Langton, 'Introduction: culture wars', in Michele Grossman (ed), *Blacklines*, Melbourne, 2003, p 91.
7   Ian Anderson, 'Black bit, white bit', in Grossman, *Blacklines*, p 46.
8   Langton, 'Introduction', p 81.
9   Anna Haebich, *Broken Circles: fragmenting Indigenous families 1800-2000*, Fremantle, 2000, p 466.
10 Anderson, 'Black bit, white bit', p 50.
11 AP Elkin, 'Reaction and interaction: a food gathering people and European settlement in Australia', *American Anthropologist*, 53:2, 1951, pp 164-86; Ronald M Berndt and Catherine H Berndt, *From Black to White in South Australia*, Melbourne, 1951.
12 Bain Attwood and Andrew Markus, *The Struggle for Aboriginal Rights: a documentary history*, Sydney, 1999; and Bain Attwood, *Rights for Aborigines*, Sydney, 2003.

13 Anon, 'Bridging the divide of Australian History: an interview with Henry Reynolds', *Limina*, 2002, pp 32-33.

14 Klaus Neumann, 'The stench of the past: revisionism in Pacific Islands and Australian history', *Contemporary Pacific*, 10:1, 1998, p 21.

15 Stuart Macintyre and Anna Clark, *History Wars*, Melbourne, 2003, p 47.

16 DE Barwick, 'Writing Aboriginal history', *Canberra Anthropology*, 4:2, 1981; and Henrietta Fourmile, 'Who owns the past? Aborigines as captives of the archives', *Aboriginal History*, 13:1, 1989.

17 Ann McGrath, 'A national story', in Ann McGrath (ed), *Contested Ground: Australian Aborigines under the British Crown*, Sydney, 1995; Christine Choo and Shawn Hollbach (eds), *History and Native Title Studies*, in *West Australian History*, vol 23, Perth, 2003.

18 Carolyn Wadley Dowley, *Through Silent Country*, Perth, 2000, p 15.

19 Mary Anne Jebb, *Blood, Sweat and Welfare: a history of white bosses and Aboriginal pastoral workers*, Perth, 2002; McKenna, *Looking for Blackfellas' Point*; see eg Rodney Harrison, *Shared Landscapes: archaeologies of attachment and the pastoral inductry in New South Wales*, DEC/UNSW Press, 2004.

20 Macintyre and Clark, *History Wars*, p 47; Patrick Wolfe, *Settler Colonialism and the Transformation of Anthropology: the politics and poetics of an ethnographic event*, London, 1999, p 213.

21 See also Robert Manne, *Whitewash: on Keith Windschuttle's fabrication of Aboriginal history*, Melbourne, 2003.

22 Macintyre and Clark, *History Wars*, pp 60, 94-95.

23 See Haebich, *Broken Circles*, p 567.

24 Macintyre and Clark, *History Wars*, p 3.

25 Bain Attwood and SG Foster (eds), *Frontier Conflict: the Australian experience*, Canberra, 2003, p 4.

26 Henry Reynolds, 'Violence, the Aboriginals and the Australian historian', *Meanjin*, 31:4, 1972, pp 471-77; *This Whispering in our Hearts*, Sydney, 1998.

27 Henry Reynolds, *The Other Side of the Frontier: an interpretation of the Aboriginal response to the invasion and settlement of Australia*, Townsville, 1981.

28 Ann McGrath, *'Born in the Cattle': Aborigines in cattle country*, Sydney, 1987.

29 Heather Goodall, *Invasion to Embassy: land in Aboriginal politics in New South Wales 1770-1972*, Sydney, 1996; Ros Kidd, *The Way We Civilise: Aboriginal Affairs – the untold story*, Brisbane, 1997; and Anna Haebich, *For Their Own Good: Aborigines and government in the south west of Western Australia 1900-1940*, Perth, 1998.

30 Rod Moran, *Massacre Myth: an investigation into allegations concerning the mass murder of Aborigines at Forrest River 1926*, Perth, 1999.

31 Attwood and Foster, *Frontier Conflict*, p 15.

32 Keith Windschuttle, *The Fabrication of Aboriginal history*, Sydney, 2002; Attwood and Foster (eds), *Frontier Conflict*.

33 *Adelaide Advertiser*, 4 Dec 2002.

34 *Sydney Morning Herald*, 14 Dec 2002.

35 Peter Read, *The Stolen Generations: the removal of Aboriginal children in New South Wales 1883 to 1969*, Sydney, 1981; *A Rape of the Soul so Profound: the return of the Stolen Generations*, Sydney, 1999.
36 Doreen Mellor and Anna Haebich (eds), *Many Voices: reflections on experiences of Indigenous child separation*, Canberra, 2002.
37 Rosemary Neill, *White Out: how politics is killing black Australia*, Sydney, 2002, p 123.
38 Neill, *White Out*, pp 142-43 and 150-52.
39 Robert Manne, *In Denial: the Stolen Generations and the Right*, Melbourne, 2001.
40 Bain Attwood, 'Learning about the truth: the Stolen Generations narrative', in Bain Atwood and Fiona Magowan (eds), *Telling Stories: indigenous history and memory in Australia and New Zealand*, Sydney, 2001.

CHAPTER TWO

UNSETTLING SETTLER SOCIETY

Penny Russell

In the forecourt of the Museum of Sydney, you stand above the foundations of the first Government House. A section of raised pavement reveals a portion of rough-hewn stone, hermetically sealed from the damaging environment by a solid pane of protective glass. Before you, the AMP Centre soars to a dizzying height. But once, long ago, you might have looked straight down the short slope to Circular Quay. Governors arriving by sea in the early decades of the nineteenth century could stroll up to their vice-regal residence in minutes, and from the windows of the modest house they could watch the busy traffic of the port as goods, news and people came and went, sustaining the life of the colony. Standing on that spot, you feel just how tenuous a hold the tiny settlement had on the vast and ancient land at its back; just how tenaciously it clung to its links with the small island, a world away, that the colonisers called Home.

Every mile they strayed along the coast or inland was a mile of separation between themselves and the lifelines of food and supplies, markets, information and administration that sustained them. With every mile the strangeness of a new land settled around them, untamed, unyielding: frightening for the real and imagined dangers that lurked unseen in the mighty forests; frightening in its profound loneliness; frightening in its alien mystery.

Yet stray they did, the land hungry and the convict alike, driven by greed or by the implacable will of a penal administration. They snatched up vast tracts of pastoral lands along the rivers and water-ways; they pressed out across the once-impenetrable Blue Mountains to the grazing lands beyond; with axe and plough they hewed out farming land and wrested crops from the resistant forest; their horses, cattle and sheep swarmed out across the land, breaking up its fragile topsoil with millions of hard-edged hooves. Explorers, survey-ors and settlers strung their imaginary lines across the map. They dotted it with names that captured their hopes and fears in the new land or summoned up memories of the old. Or they endowed it with their own names – names of men, more rarely of women, who could never otherwise have dreamed of such immortality.

Wherever they spread, the colonisers enacted rituals of posses-sion: parcelling out the land with surveys, grants and purchases; naming; clearing and fencing; holding and defending territory. And then followed, though unevenly, certain rituals of belonging: the building and furnishing of homes, the growing of gardens, the bearing and raising of families, the establishment of monuments and memorials, the forging of a history. As the nineteenth century unfolded, writers and artists took new pride in showing the Aus-tralian landscape as beautiful and familiar, no longer dread in its weird monotony. The voices of children who had known no other home rang fearless through the bush, and even their immigrant parents felt tiny threads of attachment entwine their hearts. Not all could own the land, but all began to feel an equal right to belong to it if they would.

And thus, with heart and hand, white colonisers took possession of a land they chose to call empty.

The pioneer legend challenged

'Settlers have always been unpalatable subjects', writes Gillian Whit-lock.[1] Her 'always' is courageous: to many palates, settlers have assumed the fine and desirable flavour of the 'pioneer legend'. But during the second half of the twentieth century, Australian historians began to examine in a critical spirit the inequalities of class, gender and race that pervaded the national story, and to take seriously the destruction that followed in the wake of white colonisation. Under the cumulative impact of these critical histories, the pioneer legend began to leave a somewhat bitter aftertaste.

The first significant challenge came in the 1950s, with the publication of Russel Ward's influential *Australian Legend*.[2] Ward sought, and found, the strongest expressions of national character not in the officers and gentlemen who transplanted their cherished cultural institutions to this raw new world, but in the landless bushrangers and bushworkers commemorated in ballad, story and art. His hero was the shearer whose flashing blades denuded the struggling sheep, not the 'squatter' who owned them; the digger who sought his wealth in the soil of the new country, not the merchant who profited by importing goods from the old; the archetypal bushman, not the 'new chum' fresh from Home. Channelling decades of nationalist literature which had celebrated these folk heroes, Ward gave them at once a history and a legend, and thus heralded a flood of Australian history that would emphasise the vernacular nationalism of the worker and deride the attachment to Old World values that characterised the ruling class.

In Ward's project the convicts – those first, forced immigrants from Britain's overcrowded prison system – at last found a legitimate place in the Australian story. Nineteenth-century historians had tried hard to forget their existence; those of the early decades of the twentieth century battled over whether the convicts were rural unfortunates who had fallen foul of an over-zealous law, or urban ne'er-do-wells justly transported for persistent criminality. Ward cheerfully turned attention from their origins to their actions: regardless of their previous lives, these convicts were the 'founding fathers' of modern Australia. Reluctant pioneers, they had been forced to adapt to the alien environment which offered their only hope for the future, and many had found that future to be a vast improvement on the recent past. Accepting the convicts as unshakeably a 'foundation narrative', rather than a shadowy stain to be ignored or sentimentalised, historians Lloyd Robson and AGL Shaw soon afterwards commenced the detailed social research into convict origins, character, crimes, punishments, labour and achievements that has since proven an enduring thread in Australian historiography.[3]

Ward's book, and the histories produced by the radical nationalist school who followed in its wake, shifted the demographic focus of Australian history. But they did not displace the pioneer legend. Nor did they find anything 'unpalatable' about settler society. Far from challenging the motives or achievements of colonisation, they simply turned the tables on the rulers by declaring that the finest achievements on the frontier were those of the workers, that these above all had defined the emergent national character. Radical nationalism absorbed the pioneer legend, made the workingman its hero, and celebrated the achievements of a democratic and egalitarian nationalism.

By the 1970s, some fractures had appeared in the story. Humphrey McQueen's iconoclastic *A New Britannia* challenged the validity of a radicalism which he identified rather as the struggle for power of a socially ambitious petit bourgeoisie, and of a nationalism which was, he robustly declared, founded entirely upon racial exclusiveness.[4] For McQueen, Ward's vernacular heroes were indeed 'unpalatable subjects': not so much for their acts of violent conquest as for their unwelcoming attitude to immigrants from non-Anglo backgrounds. His New Left rumblings were joined by the voice of feminist scholars who observed that the celebration of masculine egalitarianism left the experiences of women out of account, and that to include them created a bleaker picture altogether. In previous decades, the quest for women's history had found heroines among the pioneer women, claiming for them a complementary if not equal place in the pioneering story.[5] In the 1970s, Anne Summers found that convict women had been brought to the colony simply to provide sexual services to the much greater male population; that their reputation as 'damned whores' tarred that of free female immigrants who followed them; and that the only other identity available to women was that of 'God's police' who imposed a joyless moral restraint upon themselves and others.[6] Miriam Dixson followed Ward's account of the origins of Australian identity but found, for each of his instances of archetypal manhood, the women who were hapless victims of their oppression. Convict men, bullied and brutalised, turned that brutal behaviour upon their wives and mistresses. Convict men might be our 'founding fathers', but their victims, 'our founding mothers the convicts', were the 'doormats of the Western world'.[7]

In these accounts, women did not share the enterprise of pioneering with their menfolk, but instead fell victim to the masculine excesses of colonial and penal society. It was an extreme interpretation, built largely out of brief glimpses of women from the masculine histories of the period. But it served to inspire a new generation of feminist historians to fill the gaps in the historical record. In succeeding decades, a wealth of primary research has resurrected the voices of forgotten women: voices of many cadences from the authoritative to the subversive, which, though they do not altogether undermine the bleak image of patriarchy that Summers and Dixson so provocatively sketched, have certainly served to complicate it. The fetters of domesticity and the punitive gaze of the law were both integral to Australian women's colonial history: but so too were the opportunities for laughter and resistance, collective action, social elitism, the assertion of power in particular contexts, the organisation of philanthropic groups. Women were constrained by the terms of femininity as they knew it, but as a sex they were not entirely without agency.

In reinstating women as meaningful social actors, feminist historians, too, had to reassess their assumptions of the innocence of their historical subjects. If women, like workers, were not hapless victims but agents of their own destiny, then they too – and not just the male ruling class – must be held accountable for their actions. Because while feminist historians were uncovering some of the exclusions and injustices of gender, others were hard at work piecing together the story of what had happened on the 'other side of the frontier' as a consequence of the white invasion. As Anna Haebich eloquently describes in the previous chapter, the story did not make pretty telling.

Labour and feminist history had exposed injustices inherent in the social reality that underpinned the pioneer legend, and claimed for women and workers a more valuable part in the national enterprise. The new 'sub' discipline of Aboriginal history went further, throwing that national project itself into disrepute. It forced the recognition that the land, so formative to Australian national identity, had *not* been an empty land, that the frontier where society was forged through the fierce tussle with the environment was also a frontier where men murdered and thought nothing of it. It upset the image of pioneers as battlers and stoics, reinstating them as violent despoilers and dispossessors.[8]

Environmental history, which had a growing impact from the 1980s, similarly delegitimised the act of colonisation and cast the action of the pioneers in an altogether blacker light. Titles like *Spoils and Spoilers* and *Taming the Great South Land* sufficiently convey the narratives of possession, conquest and destruction that arose from contemplation of the damage wrought to Australia's fragile ecology in just two short centuries of white settlement by unregulated land clearance and the introduction of destructive alien species of flora and fauna.[9] It was inevitable that environmental historians, comparing the minimal environmental impact of over 50 000 years of Aboriginal ownership with the catastrophic effects of white civilisation, should side with the dispossessed in any debate about the moral legitimacy of conquest. Certainly the land would have fared better had the British stayed well away.

Civility and empire

Scholarship on Australia's colonial history traditionally fell into three major themes: the pattern of conquest, dispossession and settlement;

the internal structures and relationships of white society; and the relationship between Australia and England, with particular emphasis on
the making of an independent nation. This habitual separation of
themes long served to contain the impact of Aboriginal and environmental history. Stories of conquest, harrowing in themselves, left histories of the complications of white society or Australia's march to
nationhood relatively undisturbed. But by the 1990s, post-colonial
critiques of race and imperialism demanded a more complex response.
Noting that 'whiteness' was a transparent category, easily ignored precisely because of its dominance, post-colonial writers insisted that
'race' and 'ethnicity' were not confined to subjugated groups.[10] An
early response to this call was the ever more ubiquitous occurrence of
the adjective 'white', attached to histories that had once been colour
blind. Initially, the tagging of 'white' men and women added little to
the analysis of whiteness as a racial category. But over time the simple
act of naming served a valuable function. Gradually but persistently, it
began to 'thicken' the category of whiteness so that it lost some of its
transparency, while the rather meaningless repetition in itself
prompted historians to ask more difficult interpretive questions.

Since the 1990s, historians have continually sought ways of
telling more complex stories of contact and consciousness. How did
a society full of aspirations towards principles of justice, humanity
and tolerance become party to, indeed agent of, destruction on the
scale wrought by the white possession of Australia? How could narratives of 'nation making' be reconciled with recognition of what was
'unmade' in the same process? Some historians, like Mark McKenna
or Tom Griffiths, have struggled to understand the 'conditions of
possibility' for destructive acts of colonisation in locally specific contexts that allow room to explore the complexities of cultural interaction or environmental sensibility.[11] Others have endeavoured to build
that complexity into stories of national scope, in books that explore
many stories rather than one.[12]

It is probably no more necessary than it is possible to tell the
'whole' of Australia's history as a single, unified narrative. But an

angle on Australian history that draws threads through all of its major and often contested themes has value precisely because it helps to break down those easy separations. In my own work I have become increasingly aware that research into social interaction, gender, status and subjectivity in Australia's settler society cannot be quarantined from the disrupting analysis of conquest, empire and nation building. I have now embarked upon a history of Australian manners which – quaintly out-dated and profoundly elitist though the project may appear – pursues an analysis of race, gender and class via the language of 'civilised' behaviour.

A few years ago David Cannadine raised a storm of controversy by suggesting, in *Ornamentalism*, that imperial historiography had become too narrowly focused upon white attempts to contain the Other – administratively, intellectually and imaginatively. The Empire, he argued, functioned as 'individual interactions rather than collective conflicts', and in these interactions could be found 'affinities across racial boundaries, on the basis of shared recognition of social rank'. Cannadine sought to identify alternative attachments and affinities in order to complicate (not, he insists, overturn) a phenomenon too often seen in unambiguous, over-simplified terms. Social hierarchy, he contended, was an additional but essential element in the history of the British Empire; 'spectacle, theatre, pageantry and splendour' were integral to the British imperial enterprise, the display that produced the empire as a 'vast, interconnected world'.[13]

Numerous critics have pointed out the deficiencies of Cannadine's argument: its artificial separation of his themes of spectacle and status from more material issues of class, race and gender; and in particular his refusal to engage directly with racial inequality.[14] Yet it would be a shame if, in contemplation of its limits, the central premise of his argument was ignored: that we must recognise the attractions of empire to individuals, and its ways of producing complicity, if we are to understand its powerful hold across societies. Moreover, his interest in status pushes historians to draw closer links between the raw power of the imperial frontier and the protected privileges of elite colonial societies. Manners were integrally associated with the language of 'civilisation' – and civilisation, as Norbert Elias observed, was the 'watchword' of Western society's colonising movement. Republican trumpetings of egalitarianism notwithstanding, faith in the ultimate superiority of 'civilised' English society was a central premise of the colonial project in Australia as elsewhere. Faith in progressive Western social organisation – civil, democratic, free societies – underpinned and justified conquest. The maintenance of civilised behaviour, therefore, was a matter of crucial social concern.

Defining polite society

If ghosts haunt the site of the first Government House in Sydney, their voices are lost in the roar of traffic. But many of the transient residents who once inhabited its walls have left enduring records of their presence. As writers of despatches, diaries and personal letters, they documented the life of the colony that sprawled out from this administrative centre. The most prolific written sources, as ever, are the products of the rulers – men and women who envisaged, and could sometimes hope to implement, a future very different from the tenuous present. To them, the value of 'civilised' behaviour as the manner of colonisation was unambiguous.

In 1839 Jane, Lady Franklin, stayed at Government House on a prolonged and not altogether welcome visit to the governor, Sir George Gipps, and his ailing wife. Her avowed object in visiting New South Wales was to make notes on the economic growth and social institutions of that colony for the benefit of her husband, the lieutenant-governor of Van Diemen's Land (now Tasmania), whose own administrative responsibilities made such a visit out of the question for him. Undeterred by the eyebrows raised at her unconventional female behaviour, Lady Franklin energetically toured Sydney and its neighbouring settlements, visiting administrative offices, museums, print shops, churches, schools, asylums and prisons with equal enthusiasm, and chatting avidly with anyone who would answer her inexhaustible flow of questions about crops, catechisms and convicts.

Towards the end of June, her thirst for information took her to the 'Female Factory' at Parramatta, the prison which housed female convicts deemed unfit for assignment as domestic servants. Lady Franklin had been outspoken on the treatment of female convicts in Van Diemen's Land, deeming their punishments altogether too light and the habit of congregating the worst characters together in the factories one of the most damaging features of the convict system. But despite her familiarity with the female prisons of Hobart, she was shocked by what she saw at Parramatta. The superintendents, Mr and Mrs Bell, did not impress her, and her poor opinion was confirmed by what she witnessed when she found the women at dinner:

> went in – all standing at cross tables – tin dishes with pieces of meat given to one woman at each table to distribute – with her fingers she laid out 9 or so different portions on the bare table & they took it up with their fingers – some did not eat then but put it in their pockets or aprons – exactly like brutes. I asked Mr Bell about knives & forks & plates – he did not instantly answer, then threw back head & body & burst into a loud hoarse laugh or fine hysterics, perfectly affected in order, no doubt, to prove to me how supremely ridiculous was the idea of making them do so. He said they would not do it – I was much disgusted.[15]

Jane Franklin's strongest disgust was reserved for the superintendent, not the women. His failure to equip them with the basic amenities of civilisation, thus compelling them to new levels of degraded brutality, was to her a sign of his own irredeemable vulgarity. In her view, such treatment would lower, not raise, the level of civilisation in the country.

Mr Bell, callously neglectful of the rituals of dinner, contrasts sharply with his contemporary George Augustus Robinson, the 'Protector' who had persuaded many of the surviving Aborigines of Van Diemen's Land to remove themselves to Flinders Island in Bass Strait during the 1830s – where the majority soon died from introduced diseases. According to a later account, Robinson would daily invite a number of women and men to join his table at breakfast or tea, 'at the expense of his own personal comfort'. There they learned how to sit on stools and use knives and forks, and thus 'insensibly' acquired a knowledge of and preference for European ways. Through the inculcation of table manners, Robinson tried to excite 'a taste for civilised habits' amongst them.[16]

To the nineteenth-century mind, manners were no mere question of form, ritual and protocol. 'Manners, – the minor morals, ... the common law as they may be considered, of social life', pontificated the *Sydney Morning Herald* on 27 May 1847, 'having sprung up, acquired strength, and become rooted in the hearts, and conduct ... of men, are therefore stronger, and of more potent influence, than all the Governors and Councils, that have ever been, or ever will be'. The rituals of the dinner table mattered not only in themselves, but for what they represented of cultural change, social intercourse and the prospects for colonial society.

In a colonising society, the cultivation of 'civilised habits' in others carried a weighty significance. Above all else, civilisation provided one – perhaps the only – moral justification for conquest. The obligation to convert and reform the dispossessed Indigenous Australian was therefore profound. Yet respectable colonists, bringing enlightened regulation to the benighted savage, sometimes feared that their own veneers of decency and civility might prove fragile in the rough conditions of the frontier and the visceral brutality of a penal society. In the midst of complacent assurance of the superiority of Englishness, anxiety lurked about the 'savage within', which might be released in this moral wilderness. 'Oh we Englishmen are by our own account fine fellows at home', wrote the abolitionist and reformer, Thomas Fowell Buxton, in 1835, 'who amongst us doubts that we surpass the world in religion, justice, knowledge, refinement, practical honesty – but such a set of miscreants and wolves as we prove, when we escape from the range of the law, the earth does not produce'.[17] When Jane Franklin arrived in Sydney in 1839, the highly publicised slaughter of Aboriginal men, women and children at Myall Creek the previous year was still raw in the public imagination – though no more so than the execution, which many deemed unwarranted, of some of its perpetrators. She made no mention of this event, either to condone or to condemn. But the sight of convict women gnawing at chunks of meat in their bare hands aroused in her an acute, and vocal, anxiety. Like the unmentionable violence of the frontier, it presented the spectre of a dangerous loss, in individuals and perhaps in a whole society, of those rules of conduct and good governance that defined and maintained civilisation itself.

'Habitations of cruelty'

The moralistic and discriminatory ideologies of the 'civilising mission' allowed frontier violence to be repackaged as a virtuous undertaking. Few saw the ironies of a 'civilisation' that masked or justified acts of barbarism. Indeed, perhaps only a minority of colonists troubled themselves at all with the moral question of their rights of conquest. Until well into the nineteenth century, the majority of settlers arrived not by their own volition but under the duress of the British legal system. Finding themselves in Australia, they had only to make the best of the antipodean destiny dished out to them, a challenge that left them, perhaps, with as little time as motivation to ruminate on the impact of their presence upon Indigenous Australians. For others, Christianity and civilisation appeared, not as virtues that they possessed only insofar as they practised them, but as qualities they owned by right of birth. The moral equation was simple and beyond dispute: the Enlightened Englishman brought civilisation to the benighted savage. The savage, naturally, had everything to gain.

But to the disenchanted missionary Lancelot Threlkeld, the arithmetic seemed to have gone hopelessly awry. Sent by the London

Missionary Society with instructions to 'condescend' to the 'capacities and to the ignorance of those degraded beings among whom you will have to dwell; while your example will inspire them with a concern to abandon their debasing habits, and to imitate those of civilised society',[18] he clung to the faith that Christian instruction would do what nothing else had done: 'Our Object is first Christianise and Civilization will then follow'.[19] Only 'the still small voice, secretly speaking to the conscience', could change the 'ferocious disposition of the savage'.[20]

Threlkeld found grounds for optimism by comparing the barbaric violence and superstitious ignorance of 'these wretched Aborigines' with that of his own forefathers and mothers, who 'in a state of nudity danced before the mystic grove ... would look into the trembling entrail of human sacrifice, ... could yell the murderous song to the hundreds expiring in the flames'. 'If Christianity', he wrote, 'has dispelled these gloomy clouds of ignorance which once darkened the understandings of our progenitors, who need despair of the same cause producing the same effects in reclaiming these sable sons of Adam?'[21]

And yet Threlkeld's manifest disgust at the nudity, the smells, the fighting and wild dancing of the Aborigines was increasingly overlaid by his horror at the callous, casual violence of the 'cruel civilized white'; at the state of want to which many Indigenous Australians were reduced 'in the midst of this civilised Christian people, who are the possessors of their land, and the involuntary destroyers of their food'; and at the civilised vices of drunkenness and prostitution which further inflamed, brutalised and degraded the savage.[22] To Threlkeld's eyes, Aborigines had received from their exposure to the colonial brand of civilisation no instruction, no inducement to labour, no models of settled and civil domestic life. Although they possessed language, culture, civility and dignity that placed them far above the wild beast, and rendered them civilisable, they could gain nothing from exposure to a brutal slave colony which had 'degraded the white to a lower degree than that of the despised aborigine'.[23]

Threlkeld had no doubt that, ultimately, enlightened Christian society alone could offer to Aborigines a chance of spiritual and temporal salvation. But the failure of his mission filled him with a dark despair about his own society:

It is written that: – 'the dark places of the earth are full of the habitations of cruelty'; consequently it may be supposed that the places in which moral light has shined will be full of mercy, and, if not, it may be fairly presumed that divine light shines in vain, and that men love darkness rather than light because their deeds are evil.[24]

Australian manners

Threlkeld's agony over the fate of the Aborigines, though informed by humanitarian impulses, was ultimately an agony about the failures of his own society to live up to the standards of moral behaviour and civility it proclaimed. Encounters with the savage 'other' caused greatest anxiety when the white invaders caught a glimpse of how savage their own behaviour must appear.

But within decades of conquest, it was remarkably easy for the majority of colonists to avoid the disturbing, critical or reproachful gaze of the Other. The impact of disease, combined with more deliberate measures, caused rapid depopulation amongst Indigenous Australians, and in the more settled districts and urban regions they tended to disappear from sight, becoming at most a spectacle of degraded poverty, easily ignored. The trend of scientific theory throughout the century, moreover, increasingly reassured colonists that the Aborigines were indeed a 'dying race', unable to become civilised, and instead doomed by their very contact with a vastly superior race. Threlkeld's anguished sense of the distorted version of white society that was, in effect, offered as a model to Aborigines could easily be forgotten amidst the consolatory clichés of Social Darwinism.

Far more absorbing to the colonists were contests over codes of conduct and the social categories they belonged to or produced within the confines of white society. As colonisers sought to come to terms with their new lives and imagine a new collectivity, manners assumed new meaning, actively constructed and hotly contested. From the moment of the first foundation of a convict settlement at Port Jackson, elite groups shuddered at the violent, impulsive, degraded and unregulated conduct of those persons on whose reluctant shoulders fell the moral and social responsibilities of a colonising culture. Convicts, assisted emigrants, Irish settlers, goldseekers, 'cocky' farmers and aspiring tradesmen, with their vulgar wives: generation after generation of immigrants seemed to defy idealistic hopes for an Australia settled by god-fearing and respectable yeomen and entrepreneurs. Such groups could serve as scapegoats for whatever seemed less than 'civilised' in the colonial project: not only the violence of the frontier, but the spectre of urban poverty and crime, the prevalence of domestic violence, the unruly behaviour of crowds, even a loud taste in dress. In response, some colonists sought to reinstate civilised conduct – with its associated baggage of deference, decorum, decency, cleanliness and good table manners – through a combination of law, education and social policy. Some withdrew into an enclave of 'good society' and tried to ignore the 'wolves and miscreants' around them.

But many began to challenge at least some of the premises on which English manners seemed to rest – the excesses of pretension and prudery, the inflexibility of social boundaries, the cumbersome clothing and furniture so inappropriate to Australian climate, landscape and lifestyle, the privileging of 'good form' over good will. 'Colonial' manners that seemed to derive closely from English hierarchies and usage began to be parodied for their failings – their feeble imitations of high-bred English courtesy, their ludicrous pretensions. Conversely, egalitarian manners were celebrated for their freedoms and, by the mid-nineteenth century, were sometimes thought to embody key elements of an emergent national identity. Again and again, the apparent rigidity of the social and moral boundaries established from the centre was forced to give way before pressure from 'self-made' colonists whose background in almost every respect could not bear stringent examination, but who were collectively attributed with the entrepreneurial, pioneering spirit that made not only their own success, but that of their colonial society.

In a colonial world that was almost by definition both economically and socially fluid, conservative enclaves of 'genteel' society repeatedly gave ground, accepting the new wealth and new power that was, ultimately, crucial to its continued survival. But though the boundaries were permeable, they never ceased to exist, and contests at the margins were fierce. What is striking is how frequently this rarefied language of social exclusion, these seemingly frivolous debates over invitation lists, reflected the language of race and civilisation that also served to justify conquest. Ann Stoler has drawn attention to the close, fluid relationship that exists between the logic and language of class and race, suggesting that 'the racial lexicon of empire … may have provided for a European language of class as often as the other way round'. Within Australian colonial society, clear continuities of language directly linked the anxieties of colonisation at the frontier with the status anxieties that lurked at its heart. George Augustus Robinson's concern to mend the table manners of the Aborigines of Flinders Island finds reflection not only in Jane Franklin's disgust at the brutish eating habits of female convicts, but also in Melbourne Coroner Curtis Candler's squeamish inability, some decades later, to remain in the same room with mayors and councillors whom he saw gnawing at chicken bones that they held to their mouths with both hands. Candler's diary abounded with references to the importance of 'drawing the line', to continue to exclude those 'not in humanised society at all' – among them many parliamentary ministers' wives.[25]

Ideas of virtue and vice, civility and barbarity, good manners and bad, were mutually produced and inextricably entangled within 'colonialism's culture', along with the categories of race, class and gender that sustained them. The contested rhetoric of manners – the assumption that human nature was always susceptible to improvement and civilising influences, or that some savage, brutish souls were beyond redemption, or that codes of civility could reflect and encourage equality rather than hierarchy – marked varying ideologies of class and politics and different degrees of optimism or pessimism about the future of colonial society. An investigation of colonial manners, far from being compartmen- talised from issues of class, race and gender, thus allows us to hold the complexities of colonial society, however briefly, within a single analytic frame.

Throughout the colonial world, as Ann Stoler and Catherine Hall have both pointed out, racial hybridities continually threatened to disturb the certainties of race, creating intense anxieties about the distinctions of status.[26] The Australian situation was peculiarly complex. Though concerns about miscegenation and the problem of the 'half-caste' child were to prove of growing concern in the north of Australia, the experience of colonisation in the south-eastern colonies was of a much more total and effectual destruction of Abo- riginal society, not least because such efforts as were made towards the 'civilisation' and integration into white society of Indigenous Australians exposed them even further to the destructive impact of European diseases. The violence of the frontier existed alongside a lurking fear within colonial society of a genetic taint, certainly – but the most worrying genetic taint was not racial. It was the penal origins of colonial society that produced the greatest alarm, and the problems of assimilation, integration and exclusion, though often conceived within a 'racialised lexicon', spoke most strongly and most persistently to the relationship between English origins and national self-determination. Seeking 'the intimacies of identity formation' and 'the imprint of ideologies of race, gender and sexuality' within the 'precise localities' and 'specific encounters' of Australian nineteenth-century society demands a complex and nuanced understanding of the interplay of a variety of foundational experiences: conquest, convictism and coloniality.[27]

Through their efforts to demarcate and order society, through their making of stories of 'nation' and the egalitarian national character, white Australians enacted rituals of belonging. Making nation they made identity, in and through history. Making history they secured a sense of past and therefore a sense of continued presence and a grounded present. This sense of belonging, too, is part of the story of dispossession – a narrative that displaces Aboriginal ownership more effectually than did the muskets of the early colonists. White settler history, in all its manifestations, is integral to the complex story of how an interloping culture, a 'settler society', took possession of this country and marked the place indelibly with its presence, in physical and imaginative terms.

Notes

1   Gillian Whitlock, *An Intimate Empire*, London, 2000, p 41.

2   Russel Ward, *The Australian Legend*, Melbourne, 1958.

3   LL Robson, *The Convict Settlers of Australia*, Melbourne, 1965; AGL Shaw, *Convicts and the Colonies*, London, 1966.

4   Humphrey McQueen, *A New Britannia*, Melbourne, 1975.

5   See esp Eve Pownall, *Mary of Maranoa*, Sydney, 1959.

6   Anne Summers, *Damned Whores and God's Police*, Melbourne, 1975.

7   Miriam Dixson, *The Real Matilda*, Melbourne, 1976.

8   For example Henry Reynolds, *The Other Side of the Frontier*, Melbourne, 1982.

9   Geoffrey Bolton, *Spoils and Spoilers*, Sydney, 1981; William Lines, *Taming the Great South Land*, Sydney, 1991.

10 Whitlock, *Intimate Empire*, p 41.

11 McKenna, *Looking for Blackfellas' Point: an Australian history of place*, Sydney, 2002; Tom Griffiths, *Forests of Ash*, Cambridge, 2001.

12 Patricia Grimshaw et al, *Creating a Nation*, Melbourne, 1994; Alan Atkinson, *The Europeans in Australia*, Melbourne, vol 1, 1997, vol 2, 2004.

13 David Cannadine, 'Second thoughts on *Ornamentalism*', *History Australia*, 1:2, July 2004, pp 172-73.

14 See the special issue, ed T Ballantyne, of the *Journal of Colonialism and Colonial History*, 3:1, Spring 2002.

15 Penny Russell, *This Errant Lady*, Canberra, 2002, p 171.

16 James Backhouse and Charles Tyler, *The Life and Labours of George Washington Walker, of Hobart Town*, London, 1862, p 109.

17 E Elbourne, 'The Sin of the settler: the 1835-36 Select Committee on Aborigines and debates over virtue and conquest in the early nineteenth-century British white settler empire', *Journal of Colonialism and Colonial History*, 4:3, 2003 (e-journal, para 23).

18 LE Threlkeld, *A Statement Chiefly Relating to the Formation and Abandonment of a Mission to the Aborigines of New South Wales*, Sydney, 1828, p 7.

19 LE Threlkeld, *Australian Reminiscences and Papers* (ed N Gunson), Canberra, 1974, vol 2, p 202.

20 Threlkeld, *Australian Reminiscences*, vol 2, p 226.

21 Threlkeld, *Australian Reminiscences*, vol 2, p 194.

22 Threlkeld, *Australian Reminiscences*, vol 2, pp 205 and 215.

23 Threlkeld, *Australian Reminiscences*, vol 1, p 51.

24 Threlkeld, *Australian Reminiscences*, vol 1, p 48.

25 SC Candler to Lord Newry, 9 Feb 1868, copy in Candler, Diary, 1867-67, La Trobe Library MS 9502.

26 Ann Laura Stoler, *Carnal Knowledge and Imperial Power*, Berkeley, 2002; Catherine Hall, *Civilising Subjects*, Chicago, 2002.

27 Whitlock, *Intimate Empire*, p 34.

CHAPTER THREE

THE VIEW FROM THE NORTH

Regina Ganter

The geopolitical imagination of Australian history has relegated the north to the margins. The idea of a perennial northern frontier is familiar in the northern hemisphere: the Northwest Territories and Yukon in Canada, Alaska in the United States, Greenland for Denmark, or Lapland in Norway, Sweden and Finland. These regions share a thinly spread population, a preponderance of indigenous peoples, a dearth of commercial cities, an emphasis on resource extractive industries, a string of social and economic problems associated with these peculiarities, and a leading role in the romantic national imagination.[1] In Australia, the focus of national cultural and intellectual life is on the Sydney/Canberra/Melbourne axis while the other state capitals struggle against the image of satellite cities. This national imagination is anchored in historiography, and I will try to re-tell and overwrite it by hovering around three turns of century: 1803, 1906, and the decade leading up to 2004.

Australian histories tend to radiate out from Sydney in their substantive treatment, with vivid impressions of how British settlement spread from that first convict colony. Keith Hancock's *Australia* makes an explicit link between the pass in the Blue Mountains behind Sydney, first officially crossed in 1813, to the frontier image of Frederick Jackson Turner, whose historical imagination saw the wagons roll past Cumberland Gap and a century later at the South Pass in the Rockies, pushing the frontiers of American settlement.[2] This image ignores a few salient counter-movements, such as the large numbers of Chinese settlers taking the maritime shortcut to the American west coast. In Australia, too, Melbourne historian Geoffrey Blainey pointed out long ago that the overlanding narrative takes little account of events as they unfolded.[3] Blainey's *Tyranny of Distance* argued that 'limpet ports' clung against all odds to the shores of an inhospitable continent, encircling it like a pearl necklace with ports unevenly spaced, long before any wagon wheels rolled in, before settlers and explorers traversed the country, when the interior seemed to hold little promise, and transport – and the strategic imagination – was still firmly fixed on the maritime routes that promised trade.

But Blainey, too, held fast to the notion that it was the task of Australian history to trace the movements of the British around the continent, and that to this end chronological adaptations had to be made: he does not mention the French claim over Western Australia of 1772 until his narrative has got the British around to those parts in 1826; the Macassan traders who visited the shores of the Kimberley and Arnhem Land (in the far north of Western Australia and the Northern Territory respectively) make a guest appearance in the Australian story only once the British flag is raised at the Top End. In Australian histories, Nova Hollandia, with a coastline dotted with Dutch names recording Dutch landfalls from as early as 1616, becomes relevant only after James Cook staked a British claim on the eastern coast of the same continent in 1770.

It is not that Australian historians are unaware of such prior histories. But in order to find significant inclusion in a national narrative, events need to be meaningful within a narrative structure: history needs an organising principle beyond the temporal. So what organising principles are decipherable in the Australian story? How, for example, does it begin? Cook's claim on behalf of the English Crown was pronounced during a passing visit on a tiny island off the north-eastern coast of New Holland (Possession Island, in Torres Strait). In itself, it might appear a pathetic gesture, evoking merely the gap left by the Dutch navigators before him, but in the story of

Australia it becomes an inaugurating event: it is centrally important for the internal logic of the story. The annual trading visits of fishermen from the Indonesian island of Sulawesi (formerly Celebes) operating out of the trading port of Makassar, were of course highly consequential for the Indigenous people of the northern Australian coasts. But in our familiar story, this phenomenon is curious – it is interesting, but a little out of place; it does not need explaining; it is marginal.

If we dare to let go of the organising principle that posits the British as the fulcrum of a national narrative, then the story's fragments fall into quite a different pattern of the kaleidoscope. What we then begin to see, just off the northern Australian coast, is an island archipelago between China and Arabia; a region of intensive trade with successive empires, that became Islamicised in the late Sung period (960–1279), where Chinese merchants set up trading stations and warehouses; one that also attracted Spanish and Portuguese empire-builders; and where eventually the Dutch established an ascendancy – all before the British became interested in the Pacific. With a flip of the kaleidoscope, what was at the centre is refracted at the margin, and what was barely noticed at the margin may move to the core.

Three captains

The excellent British navigator/explorer Commander Matthew Flinders faced such a flip of the kaleidoscope. Flinders is well remembered for his circumnavigation of the Australian continent, from 1801 to 1803. He was also first to propose 'Australia' as a new name for Terra Australis, the south land, a label to encompass both New Holland (which had by then been relegated to the western portion of the continent) and New South Wales (the eastern portion), and eventually erasing the memory of New Holland altogether.

Flinders' voyage was in keen competition with a French expedition under the leadership of Nicolas Baudin, a scientific voyage of

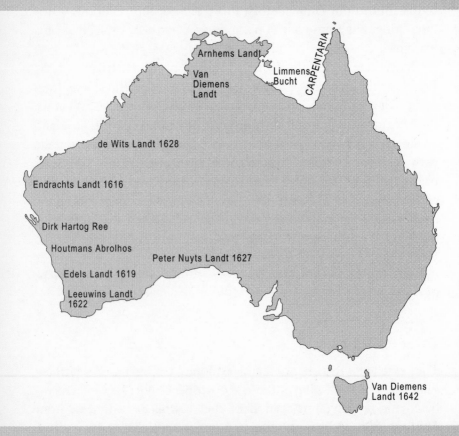

New Holland
© Regina Ganter

exploration in New Holland that the British eyed suspiciously. At this time the British colony in New South Wales was still a penal colony directed by a military governor, with two tiny outrigger stations at the Hunter River (Newcastle) and distant Norfolk Island. Port Jackson itself was not much more than a 'limpet port' clinging tenaciously by the sea at Sydney Cove, supporting a population of less than 7000. There seemed to be ample room to affix a French claim. In order to pre-empt the French charting, Flinders spent five months on the inward journey hugging the southern coastline of the continent (from 6 December to 8 May 1801) where he had a chance meeting with Baudin, who was in the process of charting it as Terre Napoléon.

Flinders' published journal of the *Investigator's* voyage was of course edited – but still it conveys some flavour of the experience of that journey. From Sydney to Torres Strait and Cape York, the journal records for exactly four months the soundings, sightings, measurements and names bestowed on landmarks with almost unrelieved boredom.[4] But in the Gulf of Carpentaria, nominally Dutch territory, a sense of foreboding developed. In November in the bosom of the gulf, a thorough appraisal of the *Investigator* revealed that its rotting timber would render the ship unsafe in perhaps another six months. Just at that time, the expedition discovered seven skulls, wreckage of a ship, and pieces of pottery at nearby Sweers Island – suggesting that non-Indigenous visitors had been there not long ago. Pointing out the shortcomings of the Dutch charts, Flinders affixed the name of Wellesley to one group of islands and of Sir Edward Pellew to the next – where he found still further traces of strangers. Broken bark canoes, constructed unlike any others he had seen, raised as many questions as did an unusual arrangement of stone cylinders. Other clear indications of foreigners were pieces of pottery, bamboo lattice-work, Chinese-style palm-leaf hats, and pieces of 'moorman's trousers' of blue cotton. Flinders by now suspected that Chinese visitors had spent some considerable time here, perhaps for the nutmeg noticed at Vanderlin Island, and that they

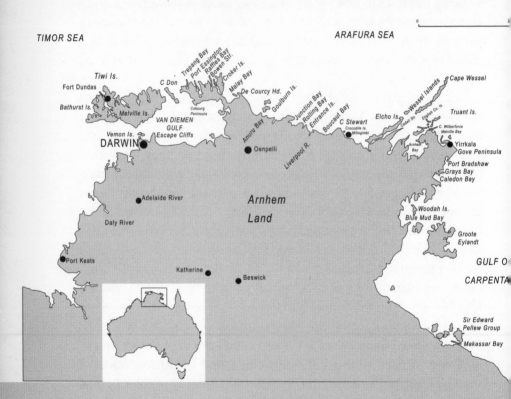

TIMOR SEA

ARAFURA SEA

Tiwi Is.

Fort Dundas

Trepang Bay
Port Essington
Raffles Bay
Bowen Str.

C Don

Croker Is.

Cape Wessel

Bathurst Is.

Malay Bay

De Courcy Hd.

Wessel Islands

Truant Is.

Melville Is.

Cobourg
Peninsula

Goulburn Is.

Junction Bay
Rolling Bay
Entrance Is.

Boucaut Bay

Elcho Is.

Cadell Str.

English Co. Is.

VAN DIEMEN
GULF

Escape Cliffs

Vemon Is.

Amuru Bay

C Stewart
Crocodile Is.
Milingimbi

C. Wilberforce
Melville Bay

DARWIN

Oenpelli

Liverpool R.

Arnhem
Bay

Yirrkala
Gove Peninsula

Port Bradshaw
Grays Bay
Caledon Bay

Adelaide River

Arnhem
Land

Woodah Is.
Blue Mud Bay

Daly River

Groote
Eylandt

Port Keats

GULF O

Katherine

Beswick

CARPENTA

Sir Edward
Pellew Group

Makassar Bay

Arnhem Land
© Regina Ganter

were not just visitors blown off course and shipwrecked. Another site he later thought was the remains of a Macassan camp, with trepang boilers lined up on the shore. Flinders also noted the practice of circumcision among Aborigines in this area, generally associated with Islam, confirming the suspicions raised earlier by Alexander Dalrymple of the East India Company.

Still in the gulf, on the mainland opposite Groote Eylandt, Flinders noticed more evidence that strangers had visited, and intensified his charting and naming activity. Three months since the carpenter had pronounced the ship was rotting, they were still exploring the western side of the gulf. The Aborigines at Caledon Bay were very eager for interaction, and to put an end to pilfering Flinders took a hostage. This caused relations to deteriorate to the point where a number of Aborigines were sprayed with buckshot. Signs of the same kind of strangers were again encountered: timber felled with metal axes, bamboo framework, and the locals' familiarity with gunshot. The monsoon set in during December, bringing heat and moisture, and as they passed Cape Arnhem the *Investigator*'s crew was in much poorer health than they had been on their arrival in Sydney ten months earlier. They finally left the gulf on 11 February 1803.

Six days later the mystery was revealed. Just behind Cape Wilberforce, still on the north-eastern tip of Arnhem Land, they found six vessels laid up and, suspecting them to be 'piratical Ladrones', approached with caution, 'all hands at quarters'. These were Malays working under the patronage of the Sultan of Bone: Bugis fishermen indeed had a reputation for piracy. With the *Investigator*'s Malay cook interpreting, Flinders learnt that the six vessels were merely the spearhead of a much larger fleet with a crew of about a thousand. Every year they took advantage of the monsoonal winds to fish for trepang – a sea slug – on the coasts of 'Marege' (literally 'wilderness'), as they called the north Australian coast.

This image of an annual invasion in overpowering numbers presented quite a different spectacle to a mere couple of French ships, which had been imagined as Flinders' only competition. In Flinders' journal this encounter reads like an unexpected chance discovery. He did, however, have a good working relationship with the British East India Company (BEIC) which financed his journey (and after whose staff he named several islands in the group he called the English Company Islands), and the BEIC had long been aware of a Macassan trepang fishery for the China market with landfall in New Holland.[5] His patron Joseph Banks had primed Flinders that the 'real reason' for the BEIC's support was the hope 'to discover things fitting for the trade of India', and instructions from the Admiralty contained a memorandum from Dalrymple (not published) referring to the north and north-west coasts: Flinders was to pay particular attention to the Gulf of Carpentaria and westward, from 130° to 139° latitude, in order that in future East India ships may find safe passage from the north-west coast towards Timor.[6]

Flinders obtained as much information as possible from the commander of this spearhead fleet, who was in a hurry to continue into the gulf before the season turned, though he obliged by staying an extra day. His name is recorded as 'Pobassoo' – probably 'Bapu Bassu': literally 'Father Nail', Bapu being a respectful address for an older man, and nails a coveted trade item.[7] Pobassoo for his part was genuinely surprised to find any other strangers on the wild coast of Marege: he knew it well, he had been there six or seven times. It was the outer perimeter of the known world. More surprised still was he to learn that in the far distant backwaters of this wild country there was a permanent British outpost at Port Jackson. He had the presence of mind to ask for a 'passport' on the strength of his amicable interaction with Flinders, in case he might meet any other strangers. Surely the kaleidoscope clicked for both commanders.

After the Macassans left, Flinders continued to explore the area he now called Malay Road until 6 March, before reminding himself of the 'rottenness of the ship' and his own scorbutic sores, and resolving to call at Kupang, the Dutch port in Timor. His journal offers several reasons for doing so, none of them as convincing as the idea that Timor was the best place to obtain reliable information about this trepang trade to New Holland (as the Dutch still called the whole continent). Flinders found that Kupang had much suffered from the suspension of trade during the Franco-British war, and claimed there were 'no merchants' there: 'only Chinese' traders and shopkeepers. There were few provisions, no salt, and the water turned out to be foul and carrying disease. The Dutch government resident basically confirmed the information obtained from Pobassoo: there was a lively annual trade linking China as the destination and New Holland as one of the origins of the valued trepang. It was not a trade that the Dutch East India Company had been able to control. Flinders departed Kupang on 27 April and made great speed via the western route to Port Jackson, where he arrived on 3 June 1803 with a crew decimated by disease. During these last five weeks, covering half the route, he executed only the most explicit instructions of the Admiralty.

The circumnavigation took ten months, and for five of these Flinders had lingered with a rotting ship on the farthest coast – farthest for the British at Sydney and farthest for the Macassans. He ran a risk to call at Kupang, a port which he knew from Baudin had little to offer, and with the crew already in declining health. The purpose of his journey was, by naming and charting, to secure the continent for the British, and French competition explains why Flinders insisted that his instructions should allow him latitude to commence some charting before reaching Port Jackson. But what captivated him in the gulf and south-east Arnhem Land were the activities of other strangers: the image of 1000 Malays descending on this coast every year. A lively trade, and one that involved China, was far more interesting for imperialists than a sparsely populated southern coastline. This discovery – or rather the confirmation of suspicions held by the BEIC – came to dominate the journey.

Flinders was unable to act on his discovery: on his return journey he was imprisoned at French Mauritius for almost seven years, finally reached Britain in poor health in October 1810 and died in 1814.

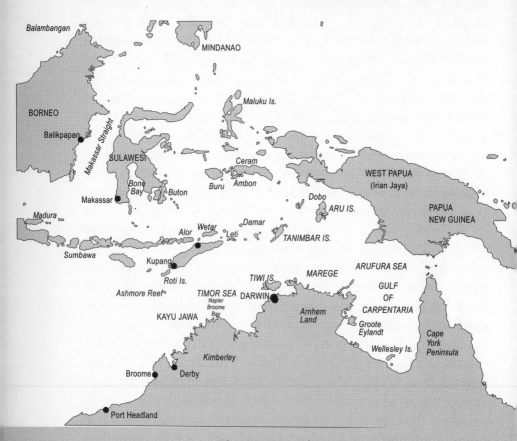

The Near East trading zone
© Regina Ganter

But during his greatest journey, the important meeting between two captains was not between Flinders and Baudin, as it is normally remembered, but between Flinders and Pobassoo.

The proximity of China

The Macassan trade eventually rendered the north coast interesting for the British. Flinders came away with the understanding that the Macassan/Australian trade had started perhaps twenty years earlier: after Captain Cook but before British settlement in the south. Professor Campbell Charles Macknight – having spent a great deal of his professional life researching this trade with the help of Dutch, Makasar and Chinese sources, and being often challenged by anthropologists who believe the trade must be more ancient – now stands firm that it must have started between the 1720s and 1750s.

The ethnic composition of the Macassan trepang fleets was diverse, including Makasar-speakers, Sama Bajo sea nomads, Timorese, Bugis from east Sulawesi, and other Malay peoples in the region. On the advice of Macknight I have therefore retained the English spelling for Macassans that has long been used in Australia to refer to the phenomenon of this trade (this collective term for a group of people not necessarily either Makasar speakers or Makassar residents makes much less sense on the Indonesian side). The earliest documentary reference to this trade judged as reliable by Macknight is dated in 1751, and refers to a Chinese trader who set out from Timor, and whose voyage was noticed by the Dutch East India Company. The Dutch kept a keen eye on the activities of Chinese merchants who were well entrenched in the trade of the archipelago.[8] They established shore stations similar to those of the European traders in the south-west Pacific much later, in the 1840s.[9] For example on Aru Island (off the coast of Papua New Guinea) the annual Macassan visitors, numbering 5000, were observed in the 1770s to leave behind 'some dozen Chinese and about 300 Bugis and Makassars' until the next season.[10]

Since Canton had been prised open for trade with Europe in 1757, market opportunities in China were always very coveted by the colonial traders because the high demand for Chinese commodities was not reciprocated in China by a demand for European trade goods. One had to be more creative, and opium from India and sandalwood from the Pacific became attractive commodities in the 1830s and 1840s – with the result that more and more distant regions became enmeshed in this colonial trading network. By the early 1800s the Makassar market traded some thirty varieties of trepang to southern China. Trepang was clearly an interesting niche market for Europeans to dominate.

What might have happened if Flinders had advertised his discovery to the trading public? Would they not have descended upon the north coast to explore its opportunities? The BEIC's monopoly was already shaken by the establishment of Port Jackson; American whalers and sealers – no longer bound by British policy – were active in the south-eastern seas surrounding the continent; Robert Campbell's Calcutta firm established a warehouse and wharf at Sydney's Circular Quay in 1798; and successive governors of New South Wales argued for a liberalisation of trading rights. By 1813 the BEIC was able to salvage only its monopoly on the China trade, and that, too, was lost in 1833. Flinders' discoveries might have turned the history of Australia upside down.

Alexander Dalrymple died in 1808, Flinders was detained, and the north coast drifted out of British consciousness for a decade until Phillip Parker King continued Flinders' work (1818–21). He also reported meeting large numbers of Macassans on the Kimberley coast (Western Australia). Soon after this, Fort Dundas was established on the Tiwi Islands (1824–29) in the hope of repeating the spectacular success of Singapore (established by the Dutch in 1819 and ceded to the British in 1824 in return for exclusive rights in the Indonesian archipelago). Fort Dundas attracted much colonial as well as Macassan trade in its meteoric rise to prominence. It was the first British attempt to establish a presence on the northern Australian coastline, even before the western half of the continent had been claimed (in 1829). Two similar attempts at nearby Cobourg Peninsula again failed to graft onto this well organised trade (1827–29, 1838–49). All of this long preceded a presence of white settlers in the north, but it directed British hopes and ambitions to the north. Finally customs officers were stationed at known Macassan meeting points in the early 1880s to at least raise some revenue from licences and duties for South Australia, which then administered the Northern Territory. Harassed by increasing levies, cumbersome regulations and changing policies, the number of visiting Macassan vessels dropped off and the customs revenue derived from them declined. Their own business interest in trepanging led those who were appointed to oversee the Macassan trade to recommend its cessation.

Bicentenaries

After a number of attempts to control the Macassan trade in north Australia, the South Australian government forbade it in 1906. At that time the trade was approaching two centuries' standing. When Australia celebrated its own Bicentenary, reckoning 200 years from the founding of a convict colony in 1788, two centuries of attachment seemed like an eternity: nothing could erase 200 years of history. The 1988 Bicentenary, however, commemorated the white presence in Australia's south-eastern corner. Elsewhere white settlement had a much shorter duration.

The north had only a hundred-year experience of sparse and patchy white settlement, sometimes advancing and sometimes retreating. The spearhead of a white advance was the Western Australian pearling industry commencing at Denham (Shark Bay) and Cossack from the 1860s. Darwin was surveyed for land sales in 1869 and the Daly River was taken up by leases in the late 1870s. Derby and Broome were declared townships in 1883, Governor Broome commenting with embarrassment that Broome was 'likely to remain a mere dummy townsite, inhabited by the tenants of three graves ... I hope it may have an inhabitant some day.'[11] His pessimism was misplaced, but we must not imagine that the declaration of a township was an administrative response to the pressure of a growing population: it was rather an invitation. The Kimberley was thrown open to land selection in 1884, followed by a gold rush in 1885, as a result of which Wyndham appeared in 1886 (current population 850, including a large Aboriginal community). In north Queensland there was hardly any white activity until 1872, when the Palmer River gold rush led to the settlement of Cairns and Cooktown – the latter boldly declared its own Bicentennial in 1970, reckoning from a forced stopover by Captain Cook to repair the *Endeavour*. But there was no white settlement there until over a hundred years later.

Nor does the history of the north lend itself to the reading of a progress of white Australia. The whole Northern Territory in 1897 was said to contain 460 Europeans, 30 Malays, and 3406 Chinese – Aborigines were not counted.[12] In 1919 Denham was 'just a small village' divided between the white end and coloured end, with a school for 20 children. Most Malays had left, and the Chinese were living at Monkey Mia.[13] Darwin's state-of-the-art telegraph line to Adelaide was hastily completed, linking Adelaide – and Darwin – to the world. Construction of a north-to-south rail link also commenced quickly (1878), but it was not completed until 2004. At the Daly River only two white residents remained by 1892, and South Australia, having poured vast amounts of money into northern infrastructure, considered returning its Northern Territory to Britain. In 1911 the federal government took over control of the territory and imbued it with fresh hopes, more funds, and new settlement schemes. Chinese remained the predominant (counted) population group in the 1911 census.

Northern histories are replete with references to whites being 'outnumbered' by Asian and coloured populations (still not counting Aborigines). The whole of north Queensland contained only 17 042 whites north of and including Mackay (21°S) in 1877, while an equal number of Chinese were estimated to reside on the Palmer goldfields alone that year.[14] Cooktown's peak population of 35 000 plummeted when gold was depleted and has now recovered to 1600 thanks to tourism. As late as 1961, the Cook Shire had a white population density of only 0.023 people per square kilometre – far less than the Aboriginal population density of pre-settlement Australia.

Seeing the past in full colour

Northern histories are often described as 'colourful'. This implies that they are not 'standard'. They feature 'colourful characters' (lawless frontier entrepreneurs) and frequently refer to Chinese and 'all kinds of nations'. Another favourite descriptor of northern townships is that they were 'unique': Broome was unique, Thursday Island was unique, though both towns had identical social and economic dynamics. Cooktown also claims to have been unique, and Darwin is 'different'. How many exceptions does it take before the kaleidoscope jumbles everything into a different view?

The engines of economic growth in the north were pearling and trepanging, pastoralism, and gold mining; and the transport industry enabled the establishment of more or less permanent non-Aboriginal communities. All of these sectors relied heavily on non-white workers: at first Aborigines and later Malays, Chinese, Filipinos and Japanese staffed the marine industries; the pastoral stations employed Aboriginal workers and Chinese cooks and shepherds; gold attracted vast numbers of Chinese. Chinese were also imported for public works on telegraph lines and railway lines, and early inland transport was by camel haulage conducted by Baluchis, Sindhis and other 'Afghans' commemorated by the Ghan train line from Adelaide to Darwin.

The social history of the north is not colourful in the sense of being quirky, it is coloured in the sense of being non-white. Cairns had its Malaytown on the Alligator Creek and its Chinatown in the central business district, Cooktown had a strong Chinese business community, Wyndham had its Afghan camp as well as Chinese shop-keepers. The result of northern demographic change was the emergence of a vast coloured population that blurred the boundaries between Indigenous and Asian communities and caused much consternation among white administrators. The predominant experience of living in northern townships was not of a White Australia, but of a poly-ethnic society.

We are one people: a northern view

Not all Australians have a blinkered view of their northern history. The Yolngu people of north-east Arnhem Land maintain a particularly strong connection to the Macassans, who are now part of Indonesia, and celebrate their shared history in ritual, song, painting and dance. Indeed, we can decipher quite clear family links between them, given a little latitude for the various spelling of names. One set of links is clustered around the family of Macassan captain Husein Daeng Ranka, whose visits were recorded almost every season since records started to be kept by Northern Territory customs officers in 1881. His father had also been a PaMarege (Macassan captain travelling to Australia), and so was his son Mangellai Daeng Maro (born 1889).

When Husein was told that he would no longer be permitted to come to Marege, he prepared to take his farewells from his Aboriginal family. These farewells have become part of the mythology of Arnhem Land. One such story is the Djäwawungu, the story belonging to Djäwa, a Yolngu man – it is published as a Yolngu language teaching text by the Milingimbi Resource Centre in Arnhem Land. This story is about the 'last visit of the Macassans' and refers to the Macassan captain 'Gatjing'. In the story Gatjing symbolically bestows on Djäwa a Makasar name and explains that a Balanda (white man) was chasing him and bringing trouble, and enjoins Djäwa to make his Macassan name known. The name bestowed, rendered in the story as Mangalay, is also the name of a Macassan trepang camp in Caledon

Bay (Karra-Mangalay, also mentioned in the story), named after Karaeng Mangnellai (King Mangellai). The story therefore affirms kinship connection and connection to place, and fulfils the function of myth – but it also contains recognisable reference to historical figures.

Yolngu men and women often travelled back to Makassar with the trepang fleets, and oral histories have turned up amazingly detailed accounts of such shared histories. Husein's daughter, interviewed by Peter Spillett in Makassar when she was in her eighties, remembered two Yolngu people who had arrived with Husein at Kampung Malaka and worked for several decades in Jalan Ma'ip (street) at the residence of the PaMarege Unusu Daeng Remba until they died in the 1930s. Like the later north-Australian townships, Makassar was a poly-ethnic city with ethnic quarters: Chinese at Kampung Cina, Japanese at Kampung Dadi, and Timorese along the creek and lily swamp. There was also a Kampung Malaya, and Husein's family was from Kampung Malaka. In the 1930s the Australian anthropologists Ronald and Catherine Berndt interviewed a Yolngu man who in his youth had travelled with the Macassan fleet and had stayed at the house of Abdulrazak Pudu Daeng Tompo, the merchant who financed Husein's journeys. He remembered by name three Yolngu who had settled and formed families with children in Kampung Malaka, and many others who were just visiting. The son of this informant told me in the 1990s in Yirrkala (Arnhem Land) that his father also had three older children in Makassar.

Both Yolngu and Makasar culture embraced various forms of polygamy. Aboriginal men who stayed for extended periods in Makassar were at liberty to form families there as well as at home, and the Macassan captains also took Aboriginal wives in addition to their Macassan families, cementing the peaceful relations between the two peoples. In the Yolngu oral histories a distinction between Yolngu and Macassan persons is often merely implicit. Husein himself had several Aboriginal wives, one of whom was also the wife of the Yolngu man Ganimbirrngu. The relationship between these two men is also commemorated: Husein bestowed on Ganimbirrngu the title of Dayngmangu (Daeng Mangngu – Daeng being an address of respect, a former royal title) and on his last visit presented him with a mast and a white calico flag 'as a sign that each had an agreement and were friends and would remember each other'.[15] The characteristic Elcho Island ceremonial poles represent the masts of ships and the strings of sails, and symbolise the pain of departure – they are used in mourning rituals.

Macassan connections are remembered in names, myths, and cultural artefacts. Yolngu language, particularly in its more ceremonial form, contains a plethora of Macassan words, including some of the most common words: 'balanda' for whites, 'rrupiah' for money, 'dambako' for tobacco, 'lipa-lipa' for canoe, even the characteristic 'yo!' appears as 'ío' in Makasar. A group of Yolngu tertiary students who visited Makassar in 1986 were bewildered when for the first time they saw the real 'perahus' (boats with characteristic rigging) they could recognise from traditional Yolngu paintings, and real Macassan captains about whom they had heard so many stories, who were speaking a strange language full of Yolngu words.

During the 1988 bicentennial celebrations, Peter Spillett organised the re-enactment of a Macassan voyage to Arnhem Land. It was the *Hati Marege* (Heart of Marege), built according to traditional design, captained by a grandson of Daeng Gassing, grand-nephew of Husein, and he was met on the Australian side by an Aboriginal descendant of the same family. John Darling captured the moment on film: a meeting of great ritual and importance, a moment heavy with history, and heavy with joy.[16] It was myth at the brink of history, the beginning of a recovery of common roots, which has since gathered momentum in a lively program of mutual visits and cultural exchange. In 1993 a renowned Yolngu artist from Maningrida spotted in a Makassar shop an antique ceramic storage pot that featured in many of his own paintings. But he had never actually seen one, and triumphantly acquired it for his local museum. In 1996 and 1997 mutual ceremonial visits honoured the grave of Husein's son Mangellai Daeng Maro. Yolngu people celebrated their family reunion with Macassans at the Darwin Festival in 1999, and at Federation Square in Melbourne during Centenary of Federation celebrations in 2001.

The Berlin Wall has come down for Yolngu people and families are able to reconnect. When Yirrtjia song cycles are represented in paintings like the one in Darwin airport, when the Marayarr Murrukundja Rom ceremony ends with the presentation of a large decorated pole, when Yothu Yindi sing 'Macassan crew', the Sunrize Band blasts out 'Lembana Mani Mani' (the Macassan name for Maningrida), or the Wirrnga band plays 'My sweet Takirrina' (the Macassan name for Elcho Island), they are not just celebrating history: they are honouring family connection. Yolngu people are again conducting their independent relationships with Sulawesi – they have broken their isolation imposed by the prohibition of the Macassan trade in 1906. Among Yolngu, the Macassan connection is the cultural responsibility of the Yirrtjia moiety representing the seaside, while the Dhuwa moiety represents the inland. I have tried not to identify individual Yolngu as living descendants of Macassans, because in the Yolngu stories it is the communities who are related to the Macassans. The Aboriginal descendants of Macassans are neither strangers, nor half or quarter of anything, but Yolngu. Yolngu and Macassans are one group – one spirit. That is the Yolngu view of Yolngu and Macassan people.

⊱─◆─○─◆─⊰

What do all these stories mean for the Australian historical narrative? Are they not still colourful, quirky and inconsequential footnotes to a much more important history?

They certainly dislodge the idea of 'beginnings', even if we take it for granted that history can start only with documented history and should not rely on myth, so that all of the pre-contact Aboriginal history is outside of its proper reach – for the beginnings of external contact with Australia within documented history take place long before the British arrival. They also challenge the idea of an 'isolated continent'. The Yolngu were well connected to the outside world, and became isolated as a result of the balanda political ascendancy – much like the Torres Strait Islanders about whom I have not spoken here.

These stories make nonsense of the idea that Asians came late to Australia. And they also re-frame the black-and-white thinking that has bedevilled race rhetoric in Australia. If we were to take the history of the north seriously, we would lose sight of the idea of 'White Australia' for the greatest part of the story. Instead of a shift from a White Australia to a multicultural one, we find in the northern half shifts from a predominantly Indigenous to a predominantly poly-ethnic society in the 1890s, and from poly-ethnic to predominantly white townships resulting from World War II, with a later reclaiming of Indigenous spaces beginning in the 1980s.

Instead of a settler society we would find a classic exploitation colony, built on Indigenous and imported labour. We would have to write a history that understands the upheavals of the Sindh and the Punjab, of the Philippines and the Malay archipelago, of Guangdong and Fujian, of Japan and Okinawa, and of Sri Lanka; and of how all these regions were drawn into the vortex of colonial opportunities and pressures, because these northern industries relied on indentured and imported and Indigenous labour.

Peter Jull observes that Australia and Canada have similar attitudes towards their 'northern frontiers': 'They often see northern regions as marginal and needing only future consideration and problem resolution, but in fact these northern places are part of a new world order'. New constitutional arrangements can be tried out there, like indigenous territories in Canada or regional agreements in Australia, 'unlike the tried and true and sometimes rather stale' southern paradigms.[17] New identity paradigms, too, can be found in Australia's north. The poly-ethnic memory of Broome and Thursday Island is not 'unique', but representational. Shared histories and hybrid identity are celebrated in myths and paintings of Arnhem

Land and elsewhere through songs, plays, musicals, dances and cooking traditions. Among Aboriginal descendants of Indonesians we see a renewed engagement with Qur'anic wisdom. As in other regions of the world where lineages have been entangled through a colonial past, creoleness is emerging as a paradigm overlaying more purist identities, such as the 'negritude' of the 1950s that in north Africa and the Caribbean served as an empowering identity for anti-colonial struggles. The Australian historical imagination, too, can be far more relevant for the future, and far more Australian, without the black-and-white binary vision that tends to eclipse the north.

Notes

The author acknowledges the assistance of the Australian Research Council.

1   Peter Jull, *The Politics of Northern Frontiers*, Darwin, 1991.

2   FJ Turner, 'The significance of the frontier in American history', American Historical Society, 1893, cited in WK Hancock, *Australia*, London, 1930, p 1.

3   Geoffrey Blainey, *The Tyranny of Distance: how distance shaped Australia's history*, Melbourne, 1983.

4   Tim Flannery (ed), *Terra Australis: Matthew Flinders' great adventures in the circumnavigation of Australia*, Melbourne, 2000, is an abbreviated and much more lively version.

5   Alexander Dalrymple, *A Plan for Extending the Commerce of this kingdom and of the East-India Company*, London, 1769.

6   Joseph Banks to Matthew Flinders, 1 May 1801; Instructions from the British Admiralty to Matthew Flinders, 22 June 1801, National Maritime Museum (UK), Flinders Pages.

7   Campbell Charles Macknight, *The Farthest Coast: a selection of writings relating to the history of the northern coast of Australia*, Melbourne, 1969.

8   Thomas Forrest, *A Voyage to New Guinea and the Moluccas*, p 106, cited in CC Macknight, *A Voyage to Marege: Macassan trepangers in northern Australia*, Melbourne, 1976, p 14.

9   Dorothy Shineberg, *They came for Sandalwood: a study of the sandalwood trade in the south-west Pacific 1830-1865*, Melbourne, 1967.

10 Macknight, *Voyage to Marege*, p 13.

11 Broome to Colonial Secretary, Perth, 30 November 1885 and 10 December 1889, cited in Mary Albertus Bain, *Full Fathom Five*, Perth, 1982, p 227.

12 Douglas Lockwood, *The Front Door: Darwin 1869-1969*, London, 1969, p 93.

13 GW Fry, *Shark Bay Days*, Perth, 1988, pp 2-4.

14 Glenville Pike, *Queen of the North: a pictorial history of Cooktown and the Cape York Peninsula*, Mareeba, 1979.

15 Ian MacIntosh, *The Whale and the Cross: conversations with David Burrumarra MBE*, Darwin, 1994, pp 18 and 22.

16 John Darling, 'Below the wind', *The Big Picture*, ABC TV, 13 January 1994.

17 Jull, *The Politics of Northern Frontiers*, p 74.

CHAPTER FOUR

AUSTRALIA'S ASIAN FUTURES

David Walker

The year 2005 marks two important anniversaries. It is the one-hundredth anniversary of the Russo-Japanese War, a momentous event that saw an Asian power triumph over a European one. Even among those who disputed Russia's credentials as a European nation, there could be no denying that Japan had leapt onto the world stage to startling effect. Jawaharlal Nehru, a student in England at the time (albeit with a greater interest in rowing than study) was among those who took heart from the victory. Among European commentators, there were those who saw Japan's triumph as an ominous development. Some believed that the 'prestige of the white man' had been called into question. Australia seemed exposed to danger as never before. Fifty years later Nehru was at the peak of his power as prime minister of the newly independent India and a driving force behind the historic 1955 Afro-Asian conference in Bandung, Indonesia. Twenty-nine nations gathered in Bandung, but Australia had not been invited to join them. White Australia, with a population of seven million people in a continent the size of the United States, was a nervous onlooker at a conference that addressed colonialism, racism and the unequal distribution of the world's resources. Australia was manifestly in Asia, but the task of being accepted as a well-disposed neighbour, an often-repeated sentiment in the years following World War II, remained elusive.

This chapter addresses Australia's relationship with Asia from the 1890s to the present – a large undertaking, making this more of a sketch than a full portrait. It draws upon a range of sources, including newspaper commentaries, popular novels and scholarly studies that suggest some of the more influential stereotypes and representations of Asia in the period. Well into the 1960s the White Australia policy was an article of faith that few politicians dared question. The preoccupation with homogeneity, whiteness and racial purity underlines Australia's troubled identity as a white settler society on the edge of Asia. While the reality of Australia's geographic proximity to Asia became increasingly apparent in the late nineteenth century, how best to respond to this reality domestically and internationally are topics that still attract spirited debate and some political acrimony.

The role that Asia might play in Australia's future has attracted sustained attention from the 1880s. Alfred Deakin, a political visionary from Victoria (and prime minister on three occasions between 1901 and 1910) visited India in 1890 to study the benefits of irrigation. Deakin wrote two books on India, *Temple and Tomb in India*, which took another of his enthusiasms – religion – as its major theme, and *Irrigated India*. Both were published in 1893. Deakin was fascinated by what he referred to as 'antique' India – the source, he believed, of all 'the vital elements of our knowledge and civilization'. Deakin maintained that proximity and shared roots in Aryan civilisation required Australian colonists to see themselves as part of 'Austral-Asia' or 'Southern Asia', adding that Australia's future would be strongly influenced by its geographical location. Deakin forecast the growth of Asian influences on Australia's future and speculated that proximity gave Australians the opportunity to know Asia better than was the case for other Europeans. Deakin took a relatively benign view of Australia's proximity to Asia in the 1890s, but when Japan defeated Russia he became much more concerned about Australia's vulnerable defences and its under-populated north.

The vital importance of Asia to Australia's future was at once more apparent and more powerfully expressed in Charles Pearson's *National Life and Character: A Forecast*, also published in 1893 – a bumper year for Asianist speculation. Pearson was a distinguished

Oxford graduate and historian who had moved to the Australian colonies in the 1870s. He went on to become an authority on education policy as both minister for education in the Victorian parliament and later as principal of one of Melbourne's leading private schools for girls. Pearson's book was very widely reviewed in Britain and North America, and was discussed at the highest levels. Britain's elder statesman, William Gladstone, and America's formidable Theodore Roosevelt both had a high opinion of the depth and originality of Pearson's sombre forecast. In essence, Pearson maintained that the European races had reached the limit of their territorial expansion and that Asian nations, particularly China, would become a major force in world affairs. Pearson foretold a decline in European power and prestige.

The influential British journal, *The Athenaeum*, was certainly struck by Pearson's arresting predictions, noting that he was an author whose 'point of view' was considerably influenced by his antipodean location. *The Athenaeum* maintained that Pearson was struck more forcibly than a resident of London or Paris might have been by 'the growth of Chinese power', noting that in Pearson's forecast 'Europe loses altogether the precedence it has always enjoyed. It appears here not only as the smallest, but also as the least important continent, nor is it allowed even that kind of theoretical precedence, which might come from historical greatness.'[1]

When viewed from an Australian perspective, Asia loomed very large indeed, whereas Europe shrank appreciably in size and cultural power. These changes were accompanied by a realisation that the world was simultaneously growing smaller and more inter-dependent, bringing Asia even closer to Australia. It followed from Pearson's analysis that Australians were positioned to see the rise of Asia more clearly than was the case for any other European nation. Pearson's book strengthened and popularised the idea that geography had cast Asia, the world's most populous region, and Australia, its emptiest inhabitable continent, as rivals in what was routinely depicted as the ongoing struggle for power between East and West.

In this story, Australia's conduct towards Asia would not only have a profound influence upon its own future, it might also help determine the fate of Europe itself. The rise of Asia appeared to give empty Australia a much greater significance in world affairs than in a world in which European dominance went unchallenged. One of the most influential books of the decade had joined the future of populous Asia with that of 'empty' Australia.

Pearson's influence spread to Germany where it was said that reading *National Life and Character* contributed to Kaiser Wilhelm's famous warning about the 'yellow peril'. Seized by the danger supposedly emanating from the East, Wilhelm drew a sketch of the confrontation between East and West that Professor Knackfuss turned into an allegorical painting titled 'The Yellow Peril'. The painting caused a sensation in Europe and its fame spread when Wilhelm sent it to St Petersburg as a gift to the Tsar. The painting depicts an archangel leading a group of female personifications of the nations of Europe (Germania to the fore and Britannia holding back) towards a river, possibly the Danube. On the opposite bank the threatening East gathers its forces amid fire, storm and the inevitable dragon.[2] The 'yellow peril' had found a name and had begun its remarkable career with a little help from a scholarly Melbournian – not that Pearson was aware of his impact in Germany. He had died in 1894, the year before Professor Knackfuss completed his painting.

While Pearson's book was scholarly, closely argued and carefully footnoted, concern about the rise of Asia was also an ideal subject for the cloak-and-dagger world of popular fiction. Alongside the yellow peril and elaborating its dire potentialities, there emerged a range of evilly disposed characters determined to destroy the West and its influence. The most remarkable and enduring creation of them all was Sax Rohmer's 'Dr Fu Manchu' who began his fictional career in 1913. The doctor's origins are not clear, but there were several Australian authors who provided possible precursors for Fu Manchu. This is hardly very surprising given the important role assigned to demonic Asia in *fin-de-siècle* Australia. Perhaps the closest prototype is the dark and mesmeric Dr Nikola, the creation of the Australian expatriate writer, Guy Boothby. Boothby poured out seven Nikola novels between 1895 (*A Bid for Fortune*) and 1902 (*The Curse of the Snake*) with astonishing fluency and a fine disregard for consistent story lines. Nikola exuded a mysteriously Eastern character and had certainly spent a good deal of his time in the orient, but he comes closest to Fu Manchu in his genius for futuristic medical experiments. It was Nikola's boast that he had 'acquired all the knowledge that modern science has accumulated' just as he had explored and tested 'the magic of the East to the uttermost'.[3]

In 1910, three years before Dr Fu Manchu's chilling debut, Albert Dorrington, another expatriate Australian novelist in the Boothby mould, created Doctor Tsarka, a sinister Japanese 'nerve specialist'. What could be more appropriate in 1910? Dorrington's *The Radium Terrors* brought together the fascination with *japonisme* and the mounting concern that modern industrial life caused new and troubling nervous disorders, thereby hastening the racial decay of the West (or as Theodore Roosevelt preferred to describe it, 'race suicide'). Tsarka displayed many of the attributes common to the oriental masterminds of popular fiction. Although physically unprepossessing – more shrunken elf than human – he had a mighty brain. On his first meeting with Tsarka, the hero of *The Radium Terrors* 'felt instinctively that he was under the surveillance of a master criminal, a man frail of body, but whose very presence exuded the Titanic energies of his mind'.[4] As a trio, Drs Nikola, Tsarka and Fu Manchu possessed some of the finest brains on the planet, but each turned his energies to criminal ends. For Tsarka and Fu Manchu, a determination to avenge the racial humiliations of the past was a powerful motivating force.

Popular fiction elaborated characteristics that lent a special menace to the rise of Asia. The 'mind' of the East held particular terrors. Readers were led to believe that it was difficult to fathom, working as it did to a logic that baffled and eluded the West; it drew upon arcane traditions of mind control and mesmeric enhancement; it was drawn as naturally to evil purposes as the Christian West was to the greater good; it had little regard for truth and honesty, and was twisted by anger and resentment. There was also something ominous for a newly minted society like Australia's in a potential conflict with cultures that were thought of as old, devious and subtle. These were formidable characteristics in an adversary made more so by another attribute freely associated with the East, namely infinite patience. The East was said to have an inexhaustible capacity for patiently planning the downfall of its enemies. Australia was positioned near the opposite end of this admittedly contrived spectrum. The huge brain in a shrunken body was not as recognisably Australian as its reverse, muscled manhood, largely untrammelled by brainpower. It seemed reasonable to fear for the future of a young, innocent and unworldly culture set adrift in the perilous waters of the mysterious East.

If the cleverness attributed to the devious East was considered something that Australia would have to guard against, so too was the belief that proximity to Asia accentuated the danger of disease and racial contamination. Historians have paid a good deal of attention to the ways in which the Australian continent has been conceptualised as a place and a space free of disease, a land capable of attaining racial purity. In his pioneering comparative study of race relations, *Fear and Hatred: Purifying Australia and California 1850–1901*, Andrew Markus demonstrated that by linking dirt, disease and immorality to the Chinese it became much easier to ostracise them and legislate against their presence in the colonies. There was a presumption that Australia was a continent without disease, a status it could not hope to maintain if the Chinese were permitted to continue settling in the colonies.

In a recent case-study of a smallpox scare in colonial New South Wales in 1881–82, Greg Watters has shown that a European source for the disease was much more probable than a Chinese one. But for a struggling colonial premier determined to exploit the politics of exclusion, blaming the Chinese was too good an opportunity to overlook.[5] While Sydney's leading daily newspaper, the *Sydney Morning Herald*, was no great friend of the Chinese, it was nonetheless critical of a government that had gone out of its way to manipulate anti-Chinese sentiment. The ideal of a White Australia won overwhelming support in late nineteenth-century Australia and was applauded on several grounds, not least that Australia had to be kept free from what was considered Asian contamination. The popular writer, entrepreneur and politician, Randolph Bedford, captured mainstream opinion when he declared that it was Australia's 'sacred duty' to breed a 'pure race in a clean continent'.[6] A fear of 'Asian' dirt and contamination informed Bedford's conceptualisation of Australia's future. We might also note that Sax Rohmer represented the contest between Dr Fu Manchu and his adversary Sir Denis Nayland Smith as a war between the 'insidious' orient and 'clean British efficiency'. Racial mixing was certainly considered dangerously unclean and detrimental to the future of white Australia.

Alison Bashford has refined our understanding of the relationship between exclusionary legislation and the surveillance of disease through quarantine measures from the late nineteenth century onwards. The making of a clean, racially pure White Australia was considered a bold experiment in 'race-building'. 'Part of the effect of joint infectious disease and immigration regulation over the twentieth century', Bashford writes, 'has been the imagining, as well as the technical implementation of the island-nation as ostensibly secure, racially and territorially.'[7] As Ien Ang has written, the carefully constructed understanding of Australia as an island-continent provided the 'fledgling settler society with a singular sense of spatial identity, the integrity of which coincided with that of the whole island-continent'.[8] The current preoccupation with border protection in Australia, particularly since 11 September 2001, is linked conceptually and historically to a process of separating Australia from Asia - although the Australia of 2001 was a very different society from the newly federated Commonwealth of 1901. Even so, the intensified naval surveillance of Australia's northern waters in recent years and the criminalisation of Indonesian fishermen affirm Australia's continuing sensitivity over its northern borders.

Australia's proximity to Asia has also been seen as a bonus. Where some talked of invasion and vulnerability, others saw rapidly expanding markets for Australian products. Before World War I, a prophet of the new doctrine of trade with Asia predicted that Japan would become Australia's major trading partner. In the 1930s, Japan had become the second largest buyer of Australian wool, but its rapid industrialisation after World War II brought a steady increase in trade. By the late 1960s Japan had fulfilled the prediction made half a century earlier. In 1910 a prominent Australian commercial figure with considerable Asian experience likewise predicted that Australia's commercial and cultural future lay in Asia. He argued for the teaching of Asian languages in Australian universities to equip the rising generation of Australians with the languages and cultural skills they would need in order to make the most of Australia's favourable position in Asia.[9] Even when anxiety about Australia's proximity to Asia was at its height, there were optimistic accounts of the benefits to be derived from proximity to Asia and particularly to Asian markets.

Nonetheless, while there were those like the English travel writer and commentator, John Foster Fraser, who wrote of Australia in 1910 as 'an eastern country inhabited by men from the west', the business of separating Australia from Asia was more common before World War II – and especially so among the more fervent Australian nationalists.[10] Randolph Bedford was particularly incensed by any suggestion that Australia was part of Asia, an argument often supported by reference to the heat and tropical conditions that supposedly connected Australia with the countries to its north. The portly Bedford acquired a dangerously hypertensive hue at the merest whisper of this heresy, announcing that whereas Asian heat was enervating, producing limp and fibreless 'natives', Australian heat was invigorating and vital to the cause of Anglo-Saxon racial renewal. In Bedford's view Australia would not produce a race of washed out, orientalised whites but a new and superior racial type, prefigured in the sturdy pioneers of outback Australia.

Whether the predictions about Australia's future were sombre, as in Charles Pearson's case, or boastfully optimistic as in Randolph Bedford's, it remains true that at the point when it became a new and (largely) independent nation in 1901 Australia was prey to a measure of 'survivalist anxiety'. Would a nation with such a small population in such a large and largely empty continent be able to survive, even be permitted to survive, given its precarious position on the edge of 'land hungry' Asia? If it could be done, was it morally right for a privileged handful of prosperous whites to keep an entire continent to themselves? (These questions are addressed more fully in my book *Anxious Nation*.[11])

The idea that Asia might invade Australia, while simple enough on the surface, served a variety of ends, among them the need to arouse geographically dispersed settlers to a sense of common purpose. Imagining that Australia might become 'Asian' was one way of fostering the Australian characteristics that would best serve the interests of national self-preservation. At a time when the female franchise and the new woman attracted increasing notice, the fear of Asia was commonly invoked as a reminder that manly values and the soldierly skills of horsemanship, sharp-shooting and knowledge of the land might serve Australia better than the progressive views attributed to urban intellectuals. For the anti-Asian and assertively nationalist *Bulletin* magazine, established in 1880 as the voice of the new Australia, the bushman of the dry interior displayed the qualities the new Commonwealth would need if it were to survive as a free nation in a dangerous world. Resisting Asia, keeping Asia at a distance, was a masculine responsibility culturally encoded in late nineteenth-century understandings of the protective role expected of the male. The Australian male was imagined as a warrior in waiting, harbouring his energies and preserving his strengths in the event of a challenge from the north. He may have lived in the city, but his spirit was said to dwell in the unprotected regions of the continent. In short, bush values were recruited to serve an anti-Asian cause.

Australia's proximity to Asia also served some important literary ends not least because it provided fresh themes for writers and journalists. Invasion stories had found favour with British readers from the 1870s when *Blackwood's Magazine* serialised *The Battle of Dorking*, and in doing so helped create a new genre. British historian, Daniel Pick, has written illuminatingly of the multiple cultural, social and political purposes served by late nineteenth-century invasion scares in Britain.[12] A threatened nation provides a rich speculative terrain for writers and social critics, an opportunity to define national goals and identify strengths and weaknesses in the 'life and character' of the nation. If proximity to Asia made Australia appear more threatened, it also increased the drama and excitement of Australian lives. Similarly, if Asia was viewed as the centre of a coming world conflict, it followed that Australia was at the cutting edge of the global struggle for racial supremacy rather than an insignificant spot on the remote periphery of the British Empire.

The discovery of proximate Asia coincided with a growing commentary on how rapidly the world was shrinking with the impact of new technologies, especially in transport and communication. Tourism had shortened and domesticated the trip to Asia. In the late 1880s Henry Parkes, the ageing premier of New South Wales, who had known the rigours of the voyage to Australia earlier in the century, commented that Asia was a mere 'tourist trip' from Australia. In Ambrose Pratt's *The Big Five* – a fictional account of an Asian colony in northern Australia published in 1910 – Asia is represented as a landmass just over the horizon from Darwin. Lieutenant-Colonel Eldred Pottinger addressed some of the consequences of a world grown smaller and more inter-dependent in a series of radio talks in 1928. Pottinger spoke of Australians inhabiting a 'shrinking world' in which the wireless and the aeroplane were 'rapidly eliminating time and space'. Australia was no longer an isolated continent and the nations of Asia had rapidly become 'near neighbours'. In this new and shrinking world, Pottinger believed that Australians would have to modernise both their understanding of

Asia and their behaviour towards people of Asian background. He believed that the starting point in this process of re-education was for the 'white races' to abandon the notion that 'all coloured people are inferior beings'.[13] In 1930 HL Wilkinson reached a similar conclusion in his detailed examination of the White Australia policy. Wilkinson saw substantial problems facing Australia in having their exclusionary policy accepted and understood in a world of shrinking distances and growing international awareness.[14]

These comments were not made in isolation. From the mid-1920s the Institute of Pacific Relations (IPR), a body formed in the early 1920s, began the task of creating a community of Pacific nations. From 1925 the institute organised biennial conferences on vital Pacific issues including war, poverty and population. Australian delegations attended all conferences and contributed to the extensive publication program of the institute. While the work of the Institute of Pacific Relations was not well known to the public at large, it nonetheless played an important role in familiarising some of Australia's leading public intellectuals with the region. Among them was Frederic Eggleston, who led the Australian delegations in 1927 and 1929 to Honolulu and Kyoto respectively. For Eggleston, who became Australia's first diplomatic appointment to Nationalist China in 1941 (as 'envoy extraordinary and minister plenipotentiary'), IPR conferences provided vital, first-hand contacts with Asian intellectuals – something that was hardly possible in Australia where the restrictions imposed under the White Australia policy minimised such contacts. While he supported immigration restriction, Eggleston recognised that Australia's future would be largely determined by events in Asia. He became an influential exponent of the view that while Australia was linked to Europe by its history, it was geographically part of Asia.[15]

At the 1929 Kyoto conference, Eggleston acknowledged that Australia would have to improve the living conditions of its Aboriginal population – an instructive admission, for it demonstrated that an issue that aroused relatively little concern among white Australians at the time might well loom large in the minds of Australia's Asian neighbours. The White Australia policy also looked rather more contentious when viewed from Asia. As a lawyer, politician and Pacific intellectual, Eggleston became uneasily aware of the difficulties Australia would face in trying to reconcile an attachment to an exclusionary immigration program with aspirations for Australians to become 'better citizens of the Pacific world'. One sign of the changing response to the region was the dispatch of a Goodwill Mission to the East in 1934, led by the Commonwealth attorney-general and later ambassador to Japan, Sir John Latham. Following Latham's visit, trade commissioners were appointed to Batavia, Shanghai and Tokyo. By the 1930s, a growing group of intellectuals had also turned their attention to Australia's Asian future. Stimulated by Latham's mission, a number of them contributed to the first major publication on Australia's relations with Asia, *Australia and the Far East: Diplomatic and Trade Relations* – a dry and uninviting title for an often innovative and wide-ranging inquiry.[16]

Popular writers of the 1930s were also drawn to the orient, influenced no doubt by the booming sales and lucrative film scripts that seemed to follow the publication of each new novel featuring Dr Fu Manchu. 1933 was a wonderful year for Fu Manchu devotees with the publication of *The Bride of Fu Manchu* and *The Mask of Fu Manchu*. In Australia the popular novelist, Charles Cooper, produced a flow of arresting titles in the mid-1930s, including *The Soul of Tak-ming* and *By Command of Yee-Shing*, the latter featuring a striking front cover with a beautiful Chinese woman encircled by a startled looking dragon.[17] Dragons and snakes continued to serve as reliable markers of the orient and its deadly mysteries. A dragon found its way onto the cover of a travel book published in 1939, *Sky High to Shanghai*, written by one of Australia's most popular authors, Frank Clune. Clune had a worrying penchant for alliterative titles, but he was quick to pick a trend and saw one in Australia's relations with Asia. Between 1939 and the publication of *Flight to Formosa* twenty years later, Clune wrote nine books with Asian themes, hammering away at the idea that Australians needed to know more about the region in which they were located.

Japan's rapid advance through South-East Asia following the attack on Pearl Harbor, the bombing of Darwin and the appearance of Japanese submarines in Sydney Harbour confirmed the proximity of Asia and generated a more concerted effort to know the region. This is not the place for a history of World War II or, for that matter, Australian foreign policy, but from the 1940s Australia's relations with Asia attracted increasing attention, subjects addressed in a two-volume study entitled *Facing North*, initiated by the Department of Foreign Affairs and Trade.[18] The move towards Asia was apparent in the 1930s, but the accelerating pace of Asian decolonisation following the war made it clear that Australia would have to come to terms with newly independent and explicitly nationalist Asian governments.

The change was apparent in the contrast between Latham's Goodwill Mission in 1934, which comprised a series of gracious courtesies and polite evasions, and its sequel in 1948. The leader of the second mission, the academic and diplomat, William Macmahon Ball, one of the new breed of Asianists, was on the receiving end of some abrupt criticisms of Australian policies from south-east Asian journalists. To growing resentment in Asia, the Australian Labor government had been busy repatriating anyone of Asian background who had found their way to Australia during the war, including many who had fought alongside Australians. Ball found that being an emissary of white Australia in Asia was a profoundly uncomfortable experience. On returning to Australia he concluded that 'Goodwill towards these people must become a national habit, built on respect for the racial sensibilities and national aims of our neighbours'.

The cultivation of goodwill with Asia became something of a mantra from the late 1940s to the 1960s. Every effort was made to convert the 'yellow peril' of recent memory into 'neighbours'. It seemed that hardly anyone could write about Asia without a neighbourly reference. Robert Gilmore and Denis Warner, two of

Australia's most experienced journalists covering Asia, entitled their 1947 book *Near North: Australia and a Thousand Million Neighbours*. The title combines a traditional allusion to Asia's 'teeming millions', one of Charles Pearson's themes, and the newer emphasis on Asia's proximity and the need for Australia to be accepted as a sympathetic friend in the region rather than a white interloper. Australia's minister for External Affairs from 1951 to 1960, Richard Casey, was a tireless exponent of the neighbourly theme. He wrote on the subject in *Friends and Neighbours: Australia and the World*, published in 1954, and took every opportunity to explain that Australia's immigration policies were not motivated by racial considerations, and that Australians were less influenced by colour prejudice than almost any other people on Earth.

The gathering of Afro-Asian nations in Bandung in 1955 highlighted the Australian dilemma. Australia was next door to Indonesia and closer to Bandung than most of the visiting nations, yet it was deemed to be not part of the region by the four nations, including India, that issued the invitations. In Asia, where Australia was known at all, it came to prominence for its White Australia policy. Australia's immigration policies were a substantial barrier to Australia being accepted in the region, yet through the 1950s and 1960s any suggestion that the policy might be liberalised threatened a backlash from voters. Tightly wedged between a rock and hard place, the Australian government made the most of its support for the Colombo Plan, repeatedly using the presence of Asian students in Australian universities as evidence that there was no 'colour bar' in Australia. The government also funded an Asian Visitors' Program, where part of the purpose was show what hospitable people Australians were. The standard itinerary, however, also included a trip to the arid interior of the continent which was designed to drive home the point that, despite its size, waterless Australia could only ever support a modest population. The message was clear: there was no prospect of settling Asia's 'teeming millions' in 'empty Australia'.

One of the fascinating links between the high policy of Australia's attempt to engage Asia and the Asian masterminds of popular fiction is the need to fathom the much discussed 'other'. In its attempts to win friends and influence people in Asia, and particularly during the Cold War, the Australian government sought to understand the 'mind of Asia'. While the Asian mind of popular fiction was not a uniform creation, it was nonetheless understood to be criminally motivated and inclined to destruction, violence and disorder. The Asian genius for destruction was countered by a European (and particularly British) impulse to order, justice and fair play. According to this schema Asia produced formidable adversaries driven by various kinds of lust – with power, sexual conquest and vengeance high on the list. The Asian mastermind was typically male, another of the dichotomies that pervade this discourse; Asian women were commonly depicted as the victims of an oppressive masculinism. The European male was often represented as the sensitive and understanding liberator of oppressed Asian women, a chivalrous figure, rescuing oriental maidens in distress.

The language and social psychology brought to bear in accounts of Australia's engagement with Asia is one of the concerns of *Australia's Ambivalence Towards Asia* by JV D'Cruz and William Steele. They found that even in the literature celebrated for its progressive values and receptivity to Asia there was a tendency for Asian characters (citing Blanche D'Alpuget's 1981 novel *Turtle Beach*) to be 'without any indigenous capacity for abstract reasoning' – qualities readily displayed by the European characters in the novel for whom leadership roles seemed fitting and inevitable. The white female at the centre of D'Alpuget's novel is more fully individualised and more in control than the Asian characters who surround her. They, D'Cruz and Steele write, are 'mired in a messy and often violent concreteness' and prove unable to escape their condition without European help.[19]

After growing public pressure and a series of incremental changes through the 1960s, the White Australia policy was finally abandoned by the Whitlam Labor government in the early 1970s – a subject addressed in Sean Brawley's *The White Peril*, a comparative history of the rise and fall of restrictive immigration in Australasia and North America.[20] From the mid-1970s, with the arrival of Vietnamese refugees, new Asian communities became an increasingly familiar, though far from uncontested, part of Australian life, particularly in the major cities of Sydney and Melbourne. Recent controversies over border protection and the mandatory incarceration of refugees in remote internment camps have revived questions about the continuing impacts of White Australia, a question examined in a recent symposium *Legacies of White Australia: Race, Culture and Nation.* While providing a history of the policy, the contributors to the symposium also examine whether the ghosts of the old White Australia policy continue to haunt the Australian imagination. Is the exclusionary mentality of White Australia still a powerful force, or has society so changed in racial composition and attitudes that no significant continuities can be found? Similarly, do mandatory detention centres ringed with barbed wire and justified in an escalating rhetoric of border protection mean a return to the fortress mentality of White Australia, or do these policies have little in common with the White Australia of old? Peter Mares examines the Australian response to refugees in *Borderline: Australia's Treatment of Refugees and Asylum Seekers.*[21] In *Dark Victory*, a compelling and thoroughly researched political who-done-it, David Marr and Marian Wilkinson examine Australia's recent history of border protection and the stormy and often ugly politics of immigration and national security.[22]

>─┤◄►─O─◄►┤─◄

The subject of Australia's place in Asia is inexhaustible. It has a long history dating back to at least the seventeenth century when Moluccan fisherman made contact with the Aboriginal peoples of northern Australia, and possibly to the origins of human settlement on the Australian continent. The implications of Asia's growing influence and power from the late nineteenth century generated a speculative literature that ranged from popular and often sensationalised accounts of invasion to more sober reflections on defence and national security. Similarly the White Australia policy attracts historians of immigration policy and administration, while also opening the way to studies of race, whiteness and power. It attracts demographers charting changing population patterns and students of foreign policy. For much of its history and despite the long-established Chinese communities and their 'China towns', Asia was considered to be outside of the Australian continent, beyond the borders. But with the abandonment of restrictive immigration in the 1970s there are now numerous Asias within the continent. The process of defining how 'Asia' is constructed and understood in Australia is integral to the understanding of Australia itself, its shifting histories, cultural anxieties, hybrid identities and international alignments.

Notes

1   *The Athenaeum*, 4 March 1893, pp 273-74.
2   Arthur Diosy, *The New Far East*, London, 5th edn, 1904, pp 327-39.
3   Guy Boothby, *Dr Nikola's Experiment*, Doylestown, no date (first published in 1899), p 40.
4   Albert Dorrington, *The Radium Terrors: a mystery story*, New York, 1910, p 24.
5   Greg Watters, 'The *SS Ocean*: dealing with boat people in the 1880s', *Australian Historical Studies*, 120, October 2002.
6   Randolph Bedford, 'White, Yellow and Brown', *Lone Hand*, 1 July 1911.
7   Alison Bashford, 'At the border: contagion, immigration, nation', *Australian Historical Studies*, 120, October 2002.
8   Ien Ang, 'From White Australia to Fortress Australia: the anxious nation in the new century' in Laksiri Jayasuriya, David Walker and Jan Gothard (eds), *Legacies of White Australia: race, culture and nation*, Perth, 2003.
9   Colonel George W Bell, *The Little Giants of the East or Our New Allies*, Sydney, 1905; J Currie Elles, 'The influence of commerce on civilization', *Journal of the Institute of Bankers of New South Wales*, 30 April 1908.
10   John Foster Fraser, *Australia: the making of a nation*, London, 1910, p 24.
11   David Walker, *Anxious Nation: Australia and the rise of Asia 1850–1939*, Brisbane, 1999.

12 Daniel Pick, *War Machine: the rationalisation of slaughter in the modern age*, New Haven (Conn), 1993.
13 Eldred Pottinger, *Asiatic Problems Affecting Australia*, Melbourne, 1928, pp 3-5.
14 HL Wilkinson, *The World's Population Problems and a White Australia*, London, 1930.
15 Warren Osmond, *Frederic Eggleston: an intellectual in Australian politics*, Sydney, 1985.
16 Ian Clunies Ross (ed), *Australia and the Far East: diplomatic and trade relations*, Sydney, 1935.
17 Charles Cooper, *The Soul of Tak-ming*, Adelaide, 1935; *By Command of Yee-shing*, Sydney, no date.
18 David Goldsworthy (ed), *Facing North: a century of Australian engagement with Asia*, vol 1, *1901 to the 1970s*, Melbourne, 2001; Peter Edwards and David Goldsworthy (eds), vol 2, *1970s to the Present*, Melbourne, 2003.
19 JV D'Cruz and William Steele, *Australia's Ambivalence Towards Asia*, Melbourne, 2003, p 225.
20 Sean Brawley, *The White Peril: foreign relations and Asian immigration to Australasia and North America 1919-1978*, Sydney, 1995.
21 Peter Mares, *Borderline: Australia's treatment of refugees and asylum seekers*, Sydney, 2002.
22 David Marr and Marian Wilkinson, *Dark Victory*, Sydney, 2003.

CHAPTER FIVE

THE VIEW FROM THE WEST

Charlie Fox

Once the search for an Australian identity sought a homogeneous, unifying national centre; Australians have more recently discovered diversity and heterogeneity. The Australian federation is premised on the existence of six separate states each with its own institutions and politics. State politics encourage Australians to think of themselves as actors in state as well as national dreams and dramas. State holidays celebrate state achievements. Museums, the heritage industry and state histories all construct state identities. The media usually features local and state news before the national and international. Sporting contests pit state against state. State identities are therefore created by politics, culture, history, myth and memory – all the things that render people part of the nation. There is nothing particularly problematic intellectually about a state-based identity. Benedict Anderson's remarks about the ideological construction of nation can apply equally to the ideological construction of a state.[1] Indeed searching for a state-based identity in Australia can complete the catalogue set out by Judith Massey, whereby a sense of place articulates the home and work place with the local, the regional, the national and the global.[2]

State identities are also created out of a sense of difference. They are built from pride, patriotism and parochialism, from successes and failures, from slights, resentments and envies, from landscapes and climate, from what makes each state different from the rest of the nation. They are partly shaped by where one stands in the nation: at the centre or on the periphery. Indeed, interest in the very dichotomy between centre and periphery depends on where one lives. As Bruce Bennett (from Perth in Western Australia), once wrote: 'It is a psychological fact that those who inhabit a perceived centre are less likely than those who inhabit the perceived peripheries to believe in the values of regionality'.[3]

Western Australia is, geographically and demographically speaking, a peripheral state. It is also peripheral in the sense that it is of minor importance: Western Australians know that the political and cultural action is in the Melbourne, Sydney, Canberra triangle. This is the Australian manifestation of what Canada calls 'western alienation' – the belief among residents of the western provinces that the Canadian 'centre', the heavily populated east, where the seat of Canadian government is, ignores, belittles and neglects them. Consequently western Canada has produced an introverted political and cultural language, which is parochial, suspicious of the east, and often separatist.[4]

This chapter will explore views from the west. Mostly Western Australians have looked across the Nullarbor Plain to the east coast to assert their difference within the nation. Western Australians have often affirmed a myth that their isolation bred a pioneering spirit and a sense of community absent elsewhere. There is also a popular feeling that the east ignores the west and it needs to be reminded that the west exists. Yet Western Australians could with more justice assert their difference by themselves looking west and north to the other cultures around the Indian Ocean. Thus looking west could shape Western Australia's sense of itself far more fruitfully than its habit of looking east.

Federation and secession

It is a fundamental assumption in Western Australian politics that Western Australia does not do well out of the Commonwealth, which both ignores and takes advantage of the west. Western Australia joined the Australian Federation in 1901 and, on the whole, celebrated as lustily as the rest of the country. But the earlier debates about federation show just how contested it was. The story briefly told is of a colony divided between a conservative oligarchy of entrenched class interests on the coast, secure in parliament and with a solid base of support in the farming districts in the south-west; and on the eastern goldfields a rambunctious population of 't'othersiders', Victorians in the main, newly arrived, democratic, nationalist and resentful of the coast. For months, while the rest of the country voted in their federal referenda, the government in Perth hesitated and equivocated until finally, pressured both by London and the threat from the goldfields to secede, it buckled under and put the referendum to its people. Western Australians voted two to one to join the Federation. A heavy 'Yes' vote in the goldfields, the north and the city out-polled the 'No' vote in the south-west.

The colonial government of Western Australia had held out for concessions, but in the end all it got was a promise to build a trans-Australian railway and a deal on tariffs.[5] These did not mollify the anxieties or satisfy the separatist spirit of Western Australians who voted 'No'. The belief that the state continued to labour under injustices festered away. Tariffs, shipping costs, the reduced power of the Senate, and the increased intervention of Canberra in the economy were all thought to be driving Western Australia to economic poverty and political powerlessness. Such beliefs enlivened talk about secession through the 1920s, despite several Commonwealth inquiries recognising that the state suffered major disabilities and providing financial compensation for them.[6]

The voice of secession grew louder during the Great Depression until, in 1933, the Western Australia Nationalist Party government put to the people a formal motion to secede from the Commonwealth. In a neat reversal of the federal referendum result Western Australians voted two to one to leave the Commonwealth and rejoin the British Empire as a self-governing colony. The *Sunday Times* wrote in 1933:

> We have what England requires, land and facilities for the making of happy homes. England is seeking what we have to give. Hands are stretched across the sea to give each other necessary mutual help. But the weight of the federal band prevents the joining of hands.[7]

But to return to the status of a colony was anathema to others. The *West Australian*, the state's daily morning newspaper, looked to an assured future as part of an independent nation, in these terms: 'Are the people of Western Australia going to divorce themselves entirely from the citizenship of our young and free nation, which we believe is destined to be one of the greatest nations of the world?'[8]

Secessionists were cock-a-hoop over the referendum result but, in a strange twist to the story, at the state election that accompanied the referendum Western Australians returned the anti-secessionist Australian Labor Party to office. In the end perhaps voters used the polls to punish whoever was in power for their failure to put an end to the Depression; the secession vote punished the Commonwealth, the state vote punished the sitting government. In any event the British parliament simply refused to countenance secession and the movement died.

Yet a remnant of secession remained in states' rights. States' rights have always been powerful politics in Western Australia, a politics played by both parties. To Western Australian politicians, Canberra had always been less a place and more a metaphor for the expropriation of Western Australia's birthright. To take some examples of the rhetoric emanating from the Western Australian state parliament: in 1942, when the Commonwealth Labor Government announced its intention to take over income taxing powers, the state Labor premier, J Willcock, complained that the states had 'created a Frankenstein monster which is gradually destroying them'. In 1974 Premier John Tonkin said that his Labor allies in the Federal Whitlam government were 'out of touch with the people in the less populated states' and that 'the federal government had lessons to learn'. But this was mild compared with the situation in the 1970s when Liberal Charles Court became premier in a state newly wealthy from a mining boom. Court would always emphasise the 'West' in Western Australia, and, when describing Whitlam's Federal government, would pronounce the sibilant 's' in 'socialist centralists' with an almost snakelike hiss. 'If the Commonwealth will only get out of the way', he once said, 'the state can get all the money that will be needed to develop the nation's resources'.[9] His son Richard, Liberal premier in the late 1990s, inherited his father's parochialism. After the unsuccessful republican referendum in 1999 he was asked what it would take for Australia to become a republic: 'I think', he replied, 'the sort of carrot would be a change to the constitution enabling us to have state-initiated referenda, that would see some powers go back to the states, instead of the one-way stream that we've seen, of more power being centralised in Canberra'.[10]

As the historian Stuart Macintyre points out, the Courts had reversed the arguments for secession. Once it had been asserted that Western Australia was being driven to penury by the Federation. Now the Courts asserted that the rest of the country was riding ungraciously on the back of Western Australia's great wealth.[11]

Looking east

That there is a sense of distinctiveness about Western Australians is a common assumption in much writing from Western Australia. Isolation was and is the key. Western Australians constantly invoke the image of Perth as the most isolated city in the world: some as a way of explaining insularity and conservatism, others as a source of pride, as if being isolated implies some extra pioneering spirit.

Two assertions about Western Australia dominated the early writing of Western Australian history and both made much of Western Australia's isolation. Geoffrey Bolton describes the first, the pioneer myth, which informed the work of the first generation of Western Australian historians, as 'that tradition which in honoring the pioneers ignores the contentious, disreputable and unsanitary features of our lives'.[12] Honouring the pioneers has also been a constant refrain in celebrations of Western Australian history. It was a major theme in the 1929 centenary celebrations, in the Western Australian celebrations of the Australian sesquicentenary in 1938, in the Western Australian sesquicentenary in 1979, and the Australian Bicentenary in 1988.[13] Premier Charles Court clearly had contemporary pioneers in mind when he spoke at a 1979 New Year's concert:

> Western Australians of all generations had done a mighty job in a short time. We came to an ancient land and made it young again. We made the soil productive and unlocked minerals for a thousand uses. We have got land, sea and air networks where once there were no charts at all. We have built nearly 500 cities, suburbs, towns and settlements where none existed.[14]

The second theme is what Jenny Gregory calls the consensus myth, propagated, she says, by historians like Bolton, Frank Crowley and Paul Hasluck in their writing about the state between the wars. As Bolton put it, Western Australia was politically homogeneous and consensual. It was a community: 'Good Western Australians', he wrote, 'disliked extremes in politics, kept on friendly terms with their rivals, and never rocked the boat … You avoided political dispute because this would break the sense of community.'[15]

These views of earlier Western Australia have not survived. Tom Stannage attacked them in his 1979 book *The People of Perth*,[16] and later in his edited collection *A New History of Western Australia*. The attacks continued in the Western Australian Sesquicentennial histories published in 1979, and the University of Western Australia journal *Studies in Western Australian History*. As Gregory perceptively noted, pre-1960s assertions of consensus were particularly susceptible to post-1960s critiques based on the real existence of social division.[17]

Recent rewriting of Western Australian history has asserted that Western Australia was never really different from the rest of the country, and suggestions to that effect were the product of historiographical failings. A more accurate picture could be drawn with better techniques, a wider range of sources and greater familiarity with social theory, colonial reality and the structural nature of class, gender and racial division. In any event, historians who argued that Western Australia was once different all concluded that eventually it became like the rest of the country. Frank Crowley thought that by the 1950s Western Australians had become 'generally Australian in outlook and in standards of behaviour'.[18] Marion Aveling thought that by 1915 'Western Australian society closely resembled that of the other Australia states'.[19] Geoffrey Bolton thought Western Australia's distinctive sense of community had gone by the 1970s.[20]

Yet many Western Australians still believe that the west is different from the east because of its isolation. Between Western Australia and the east is a north-south line of mostly impassable deserts. Between the south-west and the south-east is the Nullarbor Plain, a thousand kilometres wide. With good rain it can look like a verdant paradise, but for most travellers, it is long, flat, featureless and boring, the only respite by road being the spectacular cliffs on the coast at Eucla. Ending the tyranny of distance began when the inter-colonial telegraph first connected Perth with Adelaide in South Australia on 9 December 1877. In 1917, Kalgoorlie was linked to Adelaide by rail, thereby fulfilling the promise made during the federation debates. The Eyre Highway linking Perth to Adelaide was begun in the 1940s and finally sealed in 1976. A sealed road from Darwin in the Northern Territory to Perth was completed in 1986. The networking which made radio and television truly national did not arrive until the 1960s and 1970s. Until then radio and television programming remained largely autonomous, insular and resolutely local.

Eastern Australians can sometimes misunderstand how the west feels about the deserts. Roslynn Haynes, in her otherwise excellent examination of the ways Australians see 'the desert', writes:

> While it might be thought that Western Australians would have more reason than the citizens of other states to resent the central desert, which isolates them physically and psychologically from

the continent's larger centres of culture, it is remarkable that two of the very few novelists who have affirmed the spiritual qualities of the desert have written out of a Western Australian experience - Grant Watson and Randolph Stow.[21]

Yet she fails to understand that 'the desert' is many things: to some an irritation, to others an adventure. There are still stickers on Perth cars reading 'I crossed the Nullarbor'. To others it represents a 'beneficent tyranny'. Bennett suggests that it can cause a sense of separateness that fuels the creative juices.[22] To others again it is a godsend. The author Robert Duffield remembers a real-estate agent once telling him: 'We don't curse God for creating the Nullarbor Plain. We thank Him for putting it there to insulate us from the evils of the east'.[23]

Western Australia's ambivalence about the east began with settlement in the Swan River colony in 1829. Imagined by its founders and early settlers as a 'free enterprise' colony, the penal colonies in New South Wales and Van Diemen's Land served as examples not to follow, until in 1849 local pastoralists successfully lobbied the British government to send convicts to Western Australia. On the other hand, to early immigrants and labourers, disillusioned by the prospects of the struggling colony, to time-expired convicts and, in the 1850s, optimistic gold-seekers, the east was an irresistible attraction. And so it has been ever since. To some, local innocence is threatened by the east; to others the west is a backwater from which to escape. So in the 1890s the conservative upper class regarded gold-seeking 't'othersiders' as troublemakers bringing with them working-class politics and unwelcome ideas like democracy. Western Australian politicians of all stripes in the 1930s blamed eastern states' communists for stirring up the unemployed. In 1999 Premier Richard Court claimed the strong Western Australian 'No' vote in the republic referendum was a rejection of 'the eastern Australians who tried to push change on the rest'.

On the other hand, the author Paul Hasluck recalled that ambitious young journalists tried to get appointed to eastern states' newspapers. For years Australian Rules footballers went to Melbourne to play in the 'big league'. In 2002 the local Australian Broadcasting Corporation managing director thought the building of a new production complex in Perth might 'stem the flow east of talented West Australians pursuing a career in television and film'. Local newspapers regretfully headline stories about Perth rock bands that seek the 'big time' in the east, 'the latest in a long line of ...' bands to leave or 'yet another' band gone.[24]

Complementing this resentment is the importance of beating the east, particularly in that Australian obsession, sport. A manager of the Western Australian cricket team, who had newly arrived from Melbourne in the 1970s, 'had hardly been able to comprehend the intensity with which the crowd had exulted over the discomfiture of his fellow Victorians' in a match won by the locals. In his recent autobiography, the tycoon Alan Bond named the chapter about his America's Cup yachting victory in 1983 'The day we stopped the nation'.[25] The popular matches the political: pride, parochialism, resentment and envy on the one hand, and a secret admiration and the pull of the 'big-time' on the other. They make for a deeply ambivalent view of the east.

Looking north

In a 1995 issue of *Studies in Western Australian History*, Jan Gothard argued that Western Australia needed to reflect on its Asian-oriented history, a theme echoed in Regina Ganter's chapter in this book. Such a focus would be more sensible than the east coast's orientation towards the Pacific, would remind Western Australians of the proximity of the state's north to Asia, and would link the histories of the north and north-west with the north of Australia as a whole.[26] This was part of an increasing interest among the state's historians in exploring Western Australia's Asian orientations. As Christine Choo pointed out in 1994, the north-west coast was part of Asian trading and fishing routes for 200 years before Europeans settled there.[27]

Other writers have explored later nineteenth-century contacts between the pearling industry and south-east Asian countries. After Aborigines were excluded, 'Malays' (a generic term for workers from the Indonesian archipelago including Malaya), Filipinos and Japanese were the backbone of the pearling industry until World War II, while illicit Japanese capital controlled much of it until the Japanese were interned during that war and expelled shortly afterwards. This organised labour migration which linked the north to Asia also joined the government in Western Australia to the Dutch authorities in Batavia. The Dutch insisted on protective legislation for its subjects brought to places like Broome, and in 1875 began to demand deposits to ensure that 'Malays' were sent home on completion of their contracts. Dutch authorities also helped police their subjects, executing pearlers from the Indies who mutinied on Western Australian luggers and extraditing 'Manilamen' (Filipino workers) who did likewise to face justice back in Western Australia.

By the time the Western Australian *Immigration Restriction Act* was passed in 1897, the south-east Asian workforce was well established in the north of the colony, but later legislation excluded this pearling workforce from the south. The considerable cultural transformations which occurred in places like Broome were therefore partly due to the concentration there of immigrant workers. A racialised social structure in the north made it look very different from the more homogeneous south. As Reynolds suggested about Queensland, white Australia never reached beyond the Tropic of Capricorn.[28] Yet the *Immigration Restriction Act* reminds us that the notion of White Australia underpinned the politics of race in Western Australia, although there were many Asian workers in fields as diverse as prostitution, transport and furniture manufacturing in the towns in the south.

Paul Hasluck claims that in the earlier twentieth century Western Australians had a greater acquaintance with south-east Asia than people from the east. Regular shipping services to Batavia and Singapore, a significant holiday trade, trade in foodstuffs, the presence of

Asian children in Perth schools, expatriate Western Australians working in south-east Asia – all suggested a familiarity with the region. Hasluck and his wife holidayed in Asia in 1938 but he did not consider himself an ordinary tourist. 'The novelty' he remarked, 'was not that we took a holiday trip to our Near North but that we made a voyage into the history of Asia'. Much of what he saw transfixed him; some of it repelled him. Anticipating World War II writing about New Guinea (and writing, as Gothard suggests, from within a familiar Orientalist tradition), he described the Indonesian jungle as 'darkly green, impenetrable, hostile ... savage and impersonal'.[29]

There has been little research done on Western Australia's relations with Asia after the war. Although the north retained some of its multi-ethnic character even after the exclusion of the Japanese, and glorying in its ethnic history once multiculturalism became public policy and heritage became good tourist material, there is no evidence that views of Asia from the south of Western Australia differed from those current in the rest of Australia. Western Australians felt no qualms about the White Australia policy or Australia's interventions in Asia before the Vietnam War, and were as divided as the rest of the country about that war. The arrival of Vietnamese and other boat people on the northern coastline engendered the same emotions as in the rest of Australia. Although Western Australia's population is less ethnically diverse than Sydney's or Melbourne's, the politics of multiculturalism had much the same impact on Western Australia as they did in the rest of the country, although right-wing racism took a more violent tone in the late 1980s when the Australian Nationalist Movement burned down several Chinese restaurants. The right-wing populist political party, One Nation, too, had greater appeal in Western Australia than in any other state except Queensland. Western Australia engaged with Asia as did the rest of the country during the 1980s and early 1990s. The beginning of Asian Studies departments in this period, and a new interest in developing literary and other cultural links were some manifestations of a new openness in universities. The arrival of Middle Eastern refugees in boats recently created the same tensions in the west as it did in the east. Despite Gothard's arguments for a state and colonial history which focuses on closer links with Asia, closeness to Asia has never really made the west different from the east.

There are some very recent hints of a new public consciousness of Western Australia's place in the region. When Afghan refugees began getting Temporary Protection Visas in 2000, Western Australian historians were able to show that Afghans had a long and important history in their state. The new Maritime Museum on the wharf in Fremantle asks visitors to reflect on two questions: were the Macassan fishermen Australia's real first fleet, and was Australia the last island in south-east Asia? In Chapter Three of this book, Regina Ganter seemed to say 'Yes', but I suspect most Western Australians would answer 'No' to both questions.

Looking west

If the founder of the Swan River Colony, Captain James Stirling, had had his way, Western Australia would have been called Hesperia: 'looking west', as Stirling described it, 'a country looking toward the setting sun'.[30] For Malcolm Uren, Stirling's first biographer, the setting sun was less important that the route around the Cape of Good Hope or later, through the Suez Canal home to Europe.[31] Europe has almost always been the imagined horizon for Western Australians looking west, looking 'home', anticipating the arrival of ships bringing convicts, immigrants, royals, returning travellers, trade goods and mail from home. Western Australians have watched ships sail away into the sunset, from the royal yacht bearing away Queen Elizabeth after her visit in 1954 to soldiers bound for wars in South Africa, the Middle East and Europe, for many of whom Albany's spectacular King George Sound was 'the last sight of home'.

There is another west beyond Uren's imperial one. It is the Indian Ocean itself and the countries and cultures of its rim. Charles Court was surely correct when he observed that:

Eastern Australia and particularly the Melbourne, Sydney, Canberra triangle has for a long time been obsessed with Australia's Eastern States and the Pacific Ocean region. In more recent years the Asian countries have been seen by them as an extension of the Pacific Ocean. Rarely do they pause and look at the bigger Australian picture and see the significance of the western third of Australia looking West into the Indian Ocean and North to Asia.[32]

Have Western Australians looked west? The late Frank Broeze has argued that Western Australia in the nineteenth century was more part of an Indian Ocean trading world than a continental Australian one. Furthermore, the settlements at Albany and the Swan River represented a British toehold on both the west of the continent and the eastern rim of the Indian Ocean.[33] In 1897, the Western Australian parliament adopted the Natal form of racial exclusion in its *Immigration Restriction Act* and there were very close relationships between Western Australia's eastern goldfields and the South African gold mines. Yet apart from these links with other parts of the British Empire, on the whole Western Australians saw the other peoples of the Indian Ocean littoral as alien, in the same way as did other Australians. Until the 1970s, Western Australians had never showed much interest in the Indian Ocean rim.

The first real awareness of the rim in the twentieth century was academic and cultural. In 1954 the University of Western Australia hosted the Pan-Pacific Science Association's second conference. In 1979 and 1984, Perth staged two Indian Ocean Arts Festivals, attracting singers, dancers and artists from 22 of the 36 rim countries. Dark-skinned, turbaned and white-robed musicians from Bahrain, for example, were an uncommon and exotic sight in Perth and the first festival was a success. The second, much bigger and more expensive (it had a million-dollar budget and was heavily subsidised by the state government), suffered from insufficient attendance and finished somewhat in debt. Perhaps the festivals were too exotic for Western Australian audiences and too expensive for Western Australian governments which, in the 1980s, had their minds on a series of financial scandals. The second festival was the last. Derek Holroyd wrote afterwards: 'In the final analysis Australia was seen to be a country sensitively concerned with the Indian Ocean region and seen to be interested, not in financial gain or exploitation, but in an attempt to foster genuine cultural awareness'.[34] The already existing Perth Festival, which has traditionally showcased Western high culture but has had only a sprinkling of Asian performers since the 1960s, took over some of the Indian Ocean rim orientation after 1984.

The festivals accompanied and prompted a greater awareness of the Indian Ocean among academics. An Indian Ocean Studies Association had been formed in 1975 and held a major conference in 1979 to accompany the first festival. Its programme was a sad reflection on the existing state of Indian Ocean studies in Western Australia and Australia. Very few paper presenters were Australian and none were from Western Australia. Only one suggested an Indian Ocean focus for Australian history. John Hoffman argued that the settlement at Botany Bay was:

> Not a sally into the little known, but an extension of the run of the Indian Ocean circle of powers and provision by a small foundation which faced the Pacific, but which remained alive in its crucial founding years by ties of supplies from the Cape to the Indies.[35]

Apart from Broeze's writing this is not a view that has won much currency in Australia.

Academic interest quickened in the 1980s and 1990s at the same time as the Federal government established defence facilities near Perth. In 1987, with federal and state government money, Curtin University established its Centre for Indian Ocean Regional Studies and in 1995 its Indian Ocean Centre. In 1995, the University of Western Australia and Curtin established the Centre for Indian Ocean Peace Studies. In 1999 the Western Australian Museum established Indian Ocean Week. The mayor of Fremantle wrote in a conference journal in 1999: 'One of my visions for Fremantle is that it will become the trade, commerce, research and conference centre for the Indian Ocean Region'.[36]

It hasn't! Most of these initiatives were part of what Ken McPherson of Curtin University calls the 'great Indian Ocean buzz', which was associated with the Hawke and Keating Labor governments, and which faded after 1996 when the conservative Howard government turned its attention to the Pacific, Asia and, of course, the United States. Academic interested waned as funding for these ventures dried up. However, the view west from Western Australia has been re-invigorated somewhat with the opening of Fremantle's new Maritime Museum, which foregrounds a display of the ancient world of Indian Ocean trade and cultures. It is a small display, not well integrated into the rest of the museum – the centrepiece of which is Bond's all-conquering yacht *Australia 2* – but it represents a public recognition of the state's place in the Indian Ocean rim.

>-+◆-○-◆+-<

In 1992 Alison Broinowski wrote that Australians had never come to terms with their geography, that they had chosen history and their European roots over engagement with the Asian region.[37] This is also true of Western Australia, but geography has had a further impact there. Isolated and distant, Western Australians sense that the eastern states and the nation do not really understand them, that geography actually disadvantages them. Yet Western Australians have less excuse than other Australians for ignoring their geography. Western Australia is part of the Indian Ocean rim and has the Indian Ocean in common with over thirty other countries. Western Australians' awareness of being on the edge of the continent is too often manifested in alienation from the east. Perhaps Western Australians should think less about the east, and instead look west (with that Indian Ocean buzz) and more positively let their geography shape their view of their place in the nation.

Notes

1 B Anderson, *Imagined Communities: reflections on the origins and spread of nationalism*, London, 1991.

2 J Massey, *Space, Place and Gender*, Cambridge, 1994, p 4.

3 B Bennett, *An Australian Compass: essays on place and direction in Australian literature*, Fremantle, 1991, p 16.

4 D Kilgour, *Uneasy Patriots: Western Canadians in Federation*, Edmonton, 1988.

5 L Hunt (ed), *Towards Federation: why Western Australia joined the federation in 1901*, Perth, 2000.

6 GS Reid, 'Western Australia and the federation', in R Pervan and C Sharman (eds), *Essays in Western Australian Politics*, Perth, 1979, pp 4-5.

7 L Secker, 'The politics of the press: a study of the conservative press in Western Australia 1930-1934', in B Shoesmith (ed), *Media, Politics and Identity: studies in Western Australian history*, 15, 1994, pp 41.

8 Secker, 'Politics of the press', p 42.

9 Reid, 'Western Australia and the federation', pp 12-15.

10 *West Australian*, 8 November 1999, p 1.

11 S Macintyre, Address to the Western Australian Constitutional Centre, 25 June 2004.

12 G Bolton, 'Western Australia reflects on its past', in T Stannage (ed), *A New History of Western Australia*, Perth, 1981, p 682.

13 J McMahon, 'Media myths in the wild west', in L Layman and T Stannage (eds), *Celebrations in Western Australian History*, spec edn of *Studies in Western Australian History*, 10, 1989.

14 Bolton, 'Way 79: whose history?', in Layman and Stannage (eds), *Celebrations*, p 16.

15 J Gregory, 'Western Australia between the wars 1919-1939', *Studies in Western Australian History*, 11, 1990, p 8.

16 T Stannage, *The People of Perth: a social history of Western Australia's capital city*, Perth, 1979.

17 Gregory, 'Western Australia between the wars', pp 9-10.

18 F Crowley, *Australia's Western Third: a history of Western Australia from the first settlement to modern times*, London, 1960, p 369.

19 M Aveling (ed), *Westralian Voices: documents in Western Australian social history*, Perth, 1979, p 63.

20 G Bolton, *A Fine Country to Starve In*, Perth, 1994, p 269.

21 R Haynes, *Seeking the Centre: the Australian desert in literature, art and film*, Melbourne, 1998, p 201.

22 B Bennett, *Place, Region and Community*, Townsville, 1985, p 5.

23 R Duffield, *Rogue Bull: the story of Lang Hancock, King of the Pilbara*, Sydney, 1979, p 30.

24 P Hasluck, *Mucking About: an autobiography*, Perth, 1994, p 100; *West Australian*, 13 April 2002, 15 April 2004 and 17 October 1996.

25 A Barker, *The WACA: an Australian cricket success story*, Sydney, 1998, p 251; A Bond, *Bond*, Sydney, 2004.

26 J Gothard, 'Asian orientations', *Studies in Western Australian History*, 16, 1995, p 9.

27 C Choo, 'The impact of Asian-Aboriginal contact in northern Australia', *Asian and Pacific Migration Journal*, 3:2-3, December 1994.

28 Henry Reynolds (ed), *Race Relations in North Queensland*, Townsville, 1978, 'Introduction'.

29 Hasluck, *Mucking About*, pp 293 and 297.

30 P Statham, *James Stirling: admiral and founding governor of Western Australia*, Perth, 2003, p 89.

31 M Uren, *Land Looking West: the story of Governor James Stirling in Western Australia*, London, 1948, pp 12-13.

32 T Craig, *Cross Currents in the Indian Ocean: a review of the Indian Arts Association and the Indian Ocean Cultural Festival 1977-1997*, Perth, 1997, p 1.

33 F Broeze, *Western Australia until 1869: the maritime perspective*, Perth, 1984, p 28.

34 Craig, *Cross Currents*, p 45.

35 J Hoffman, 'Nascent New Holland: frontier client to the Netherlands Indian Ocean state', *The Indian Ocean in Focus: International Conference on Indian Ocean Studies*, Perth, 1979, vol 4, p 3.

36 G Henderson (ed), *Indian Ocean Week: Proceedings of a Conference*, Perth, 1999.

37 A Broinowski, *The Yellow Lady: Australian impressions of Asia*, Melbourne, 1992, p 113.

CHAPTER SIX

IMMIGRATION HISTORY

Catriona Elder

The idea of growth through new arrivals has always been central to the idea of the Australian nation. British colonisers saw the Australian continent as vast, empty and waiting to be peopled. Its imagined emptiness, coupled with an idea of its newness, meant that the nation could be seen as a 'social laboratory' where progressive social experiments could take place. When they imagined immigration, Australian governments and their institutions, colonial and federal, could indulge in fantasies of a 'clean slate' and total control.

Immigration in Australia is a story about people from other lands coming to make it their home. Indigenous peoples, however, were present in Australia long before the arrival of the British in 1788. The logic of non-Indigenous Australian national identity drew upon the concept of *terra nullius* – the belief that the land of Australia was unmarked and empty and so available as territory to be shaped in the image of a British people. *Terra nullius* does not preclude the acknowledgment of the Indigenous peoples' occupation of Australia, but it denies the status of Indigenous peoples as owners and shapers of the land and community. This meant that the status of prior occupancy of the continent of Australia by Indigenous peoples had no power within the colonial system. Indigenous peoples were imagined and positioned as either a 'nuisance' or a paternalist obligation for the newly arrived British. So immigration policies were accompanied by policies that controlled and policed Indigenous peoples' lives.

The refusal to acknowledge the sovereign rights of Indigenous peoples in Australia does not imply that there was no understanding of prior and ongoing occupation by Indigenous peoples or of their claims to sovereignty. There was always a level of malaise about the dispossession of Indigenous peoples by the colonisers. The idea of immigration contains a tension inherent in the idea of dispossession, 're-population' and belonging. As Sara Wills puts it, the nature of colonisation in Australia means the settler remained unsettled.[1] This edginess is the spectre of the original and ongoing illegitimacy of the colonial project.

The dominant idea of the Australian nation, professed in 1901 and still powerful today, is of a 'white' place, a nation made up of a single people, a single language and a single culture. There is nothing particularly remarkable in this idea. Nineteenth-century nations flourished on such nationalist rhetoric. Moreover, British settler colonial nations such as Canada, parts of South Africa, and New Zealand had similar ideas. In this sense the pattern of immigration to Australia, though individual, is not unique. In keeping with this vision, we need to explore the divide between immigrants who are 'white' (in the Australian context this means British and northern European) and those who are 'non-white' (which came to mean everyone else). The place of non-white immigrants in Australia was always seen as different to that of the exemplary citizen of British origin.

The making of the federated nation in 1901 was preceded by over one hundred years of prior immigration to the Australian continent under the charge of various colonial governments. The ability and the will to both encourage and control the arrival of immigrants from selected places of origin have varied over different periods. Attitudes to immigration have been influenced by the government of the day, economic issues (such as unemployment), shifting worries about security, interest or otherwise in population growth, and changing attitudes to the idea of a homogeneous population. This chapter will look at immigration chronologically, giving due weight to differences and similarities in different colonies.

Convicts and immigrants

From 1788, when the British arrived with their convict ships, there
has been a constant influx of newcomers to the Australian continent.
For the first fifty years of colonisation the majority of newcomers
were convicts. The British government had long used banishment as
a punishment for criminals. Added to this was a more recent need to
move excess prisoners from local overcrowded prisons to a place far
away. After the American colonies gained their independence in the
1770s the main 'dumping grounds' for these convicts became Sydney
and Hobart (Tasmania). Over time convicts were also sent to colonies
in Queensland, Norfolk Island and Western Australia. South Australia
was the only colony that was founded on labour solely from free settlers rather than convicts. From 1788 until transportation ended (in
Western Australia in 1867) approximately 160 400 convicts arrived in
the colonies. It was only from the late 1830s onwards that the number
of free newcomers to the colony started to challenge the number of
convicts arriving. In New South Wales, free settler arrivals first out-
numbered convicts in 1837. Tasmania had a majority of convict rather
than free arrivals until the 1850s.

However, the gradual shift in the balance between convict and
free arrivals did not guarantee an endless supply of healthy, young
and wealthy migrants demanding to be let loose upon Australian
shores. It took quite an effort on the part of the British and colonial
governments to convince people to come to Australia in the first fifty
years of the nineteenth century. There were two main categories of
free settlers during this period. The minority category was made up
of adventurers – young men with capital, unable to make a fortune
in Britain but willing to take a risk in the colonies. The larger category was assisted migrants picked by the British government from
the growing numbers of the displaced and poor.

Both groups had to be tempted to Australia. Though the poverty
and lack of opportunity experienced by many Britons in the early
nineteenth century was extreme, and making a life in a new land was
a common dream, Australia was not the destination of choice for

most emigrants. The first choices were more often the United States or Canada. Australia as a newer, more distant and less-known colony was understood as wild, lawless and somewhere from which it was nearly impossible to return. Australia as the more distant port was also more expensive and most people would never be able to save the fare for themselves and family. It was only with the assistance and incentives provided by governments that Australia came to be seen as an option.

The adventurers, risk-takers and 'younger sons' who had some capital were enticed to Australia through incentives such as the availability of cheap land and cheap labour. Many colonial governments also had schemes where self-starting migrants were given the chance to sponsor family members or like-minded people to come out after them at reduced cost. However, the majority of arrivals were not people with capital. They were the poor and displaced of Britain. The effects of the Napoleonic wars, famine and the Enclosure Acts on the ability of people to make a living was increasing by the 1830s. Further, Malthus' ideas on over-population were starting to make an impact on governments. Though the colonial governments were crying out for skilled workers as migrants to Australia, the early immigration program were organised by Colonial Land and Immigration Commissioners in Britain, and their priorities were different. They tended to select settlers for Australia based on a principle of ridding Britain of the displaced poor who were becoming a nuisance or burden on the local economy. As Michael Cannon argues, once transportation had ended 'for many years it seemed that the British government had merely substituted an emigration system in which Australia was swamped with "Irish orphans, workhouse sweepings, ragged children ... and fag-ends of broken down families"'.[2]

The landowning pastoralists, who just needed cheap labour, were less concerned about the 'class' of their workers. Over time, however, there was an increasing number of Australian-born colonisers who were not landowners but had a sense of Australian identity. This group increasingly imagined Australia in terms of respectable independent colonies. For this group, the idea of having only the 'worst' of human flotsam sent to populate the continent was unacceptable. Colonial governors, encouraged by the colonial legislatures, began to reshape the type of emigrants chosen to come to Australia.

As with the convict program, the immigration assistance schemes required significant public funding. The main way in which these programs were funded was through land sales. Crown land was sold to colonisers and the remittances were used to pay for part or all of the passage of Britons to Australia. There is a dual character to immigration in this period: on the one hand a group of potential landowners and capitalists, which opened up the emerging pastoral industries; on the other, a working class which took up the jobs thus created. Funding of immigration through land sales made the dispossession of Indigenous peoples intrinsic to colonisation.

The initial project of Australia as a penal colony, the emphasis on independent labourers and the younger son phenomenon helped produce a non-Indigenous Australian population in which men out-numbered women, often by two to one. To compensate, assisted immigration programs tended to favour women. From 1830 to 1850 two-thirds of the migrants who arrived through assisted passage were women.[3] The Australian colonies were often imagined to be wild and debauched. The arrival of respectable women was supposed to bring a 'civilising' influence. The policy also reflected the growing emphasis on Australia as something more than a convict holding pen, but rather as a land that would be home for many Britons. The women chosen were respectable, skilled, young, healthy and single or else part of a young family. By 1850 the colonies were beginning to mirror society in Britain. The gender imbalance was diminishing, and their populations were growing from both natural increase and a steady flow of migrants. They were now viable societies and economies, though in no way spectacular successes.

The gold rushes

The gold rushes from the 1850s to the 1870s radically changed the social and economic landscape of Australia. The attractions of an easy fortune drew thousands and thousands of newcomers to Australia. As Manning Clark put it: 'A mad rage for emigration to Australia seized all classes in the British Isles ... the passions of men, women and children were raised to fever pitch by these stories of gold lying on the ground just waiting to be picked up'.[4]

In the decade of the 1850s, the non-Indigenous population of the continent increased from approximately 405 400 to 1 145 600.[5] Most of the migrants in the gold rush decade were unassisted, and they were mostly men – once again skewing the gender mix of the non-Indigenous population. However, assisted passage programs continued in this period as colonial governments tried to find labourers to replace those who had deserted for the goldfields. The colony of Victoria (separated from New South Wales in 1851) was the biggest recipient of immigration in this period, with migrants coming from overseas as well as from other colonies.

British immigrants were not the only ones transfixed by the idea of immediate wealth. Gold fossickers came from many different countries – Italy, Germany, France, Poland, Sweden, Norway, Spain, Mozambique, the United States and India. Though the numbers were nowhere near the number of Britons, they were enough for some European countries to nominate consular officials in the 1850s.[6] From the beginning of colonisation certain groups of people in the Australian colonies had been on the receiving end of intolerance and unequal treatment. The Indigenous peoples of the continent were subject to near-genocidal treatment in many colonies. Irish Catholics were also systematically poorly treated. New forms of racial hatred, however, emerged on the goldfields of Victoria and New South Wales. After the British, the Chinese were one of the largest ethnic groups to fossick for gold. The cultural distinctiveness of the Chinese, along with emerging scientific ideas on 'race' and progress, made them an easy target for British miners who singled them out as 'trouble'. There was a series of riots on various gold fields where Chinese miners were the victims of violent attacks. This violence was matched by legislation restricting Chinese immigration to Australia. For example, Victoria passed legislation in 1855 taxing Chinese arrivals. The colony of South Australia followed suit in 1857, New South Wales in 1861. Though most of this legislation was repealed in the ensuing decade, by the 1870s the idea of keeping the Chinese out of Australia had again gripped the colonies.

Immigration and national identity

In the mid-nineteenth century, the various colonial legislatures were granted self-government. As the madness of gold-fever disappeared and as local control over immigration selection increased, the majority of migrants were again assisted migrants from Britain. By 1901, the total Australian population was 3 770 000 (excluding Indigenous people, who were not counted). Of these, approximately 2 939 000 were born in Australia, 685 000 were born in Britain, 74 000 in another European country, 47 000 in an Asian country and 10 000 in a Pacific country.[7] Australia was an overwhelmingly British-derived nation. The new Federal government intended to foster these cultural and economic links with Britain.

Even though Australians of British heritage frequently represented themselves as part of the 'civilisation' of the British Empire, they also argued that they were not completely British. Non-Indigenous Australian culture or the nation was seen to derive from Britain but still to be separate from it. Percival Stephenson expressed this idea in his 1935 essay, *The Foundations of Culture in Australia: An Essay towards National Self Respect*:

> Culture in Australia if it ever develops indigenously, begins not from the Aboriginal, who has been suppressed and exterminated, but from British culture, brought hither by the Englishmen, Irishmen and Scotsmen throughout the nineteenth century … We inherit all that Britain has inherited, and from that point we go on – to what?[8]

Stephenson's idea of Australia was that the nation was shaped by the immigration of the British, who brought culture to Australia; Australia was derived from things British. Stephenson did not see Australian culture as Indigenous (Aboriginal), but as a distinct and new version of Britishness. He ignored Indigenous people's ongoing presence in Australia.

Yet despite the emphasis on, and the preference for, British migrants there have always been other migrants, though most of these were never extended the favour of assisted passage. The non-British in Australia were understood as small 'tributaries' contributing to the overall river of Australian life. The non-British migrants to Australia can be grouped in two main categories – firstly, economic migrants who arrived from about the 1850s, many initially attracted by the gold rushes, and secondly indentured labourers who were brought to Australia to provide a cheap and reliable workforce. Economic migrants included people from Afghanistan, Turkey and Pakistan who came to work in outback regions. Bringing their camels with them these immigrants laboured on major projects such as the overland telegraph line. Small communities of European migrants arrived in Australia over the nineteenth century. Significant numbers of German Lutheran migrants migrated to South Australia in the 1830s to escape religious conflict at home. A group of about 300 Italian immigrants arrived in Australia in the 1880s, settling in northern New South Wales and establishing a new community there. Over the rest of the nineteenth century and into the twentieth Italian migrants continued to migrate to Australia. There was a similar pattern in immigration from Greece in the mid-nineteenth century, though in the case of Greek migrants, the main communities were in Melbourne and Sydney.

The non-British European migrants who arrived in Australia in the mid- to late nineteenth century were quite successful in their new home, and came to the attention of elements of the trade union movement who saw them as a potential threat to jobs and pay rates. For example, Italian cane-cutters were often referred to by the racist slang name of the 'olive peril'. There was always some disquiet amongst workers about the organised programmes to encourage immigrants to come to Australia, whatever their place of origin. Though the rhetoric of a vast and abundant new land was one aspect of the narrative of the new colonies and later the nation, there were also competing stories of belonging and of the 'native born' Australian as well as social and economic worries about the effect of newcomers on the hard-won wages of the Australian workforce. A large pool of new unemployed labour could drive wages down.

Other sectors of the community were less worried about the 'threat' of immigrants coming to Australia and providing sources of 'cheap' labour. Landowning pastoralists were always seeking cheap labour. They had championed the continuation of transportation for this reason. When convict labour started to dry up in the 1840s pastoralists and business-owners turned to other sources of cheap labour. Immigrants who might fill this category were actively sought out. Groups of indentured labourers from many countries were brought to Australia over the nineteenth century and into the early twentieth century. Labourers from Japan were used in industries in the north of the country including sugar and pearling. Pacific Islander peoples were brought in to Australia to work in the Queensland sugar industry. People from India were also recruited to work as a cheaper labour force in northern parts of Australia. The appeal of the cheapness of the labour intersected with contemporary views about the unsuitability of the 'white races' for work in the 'tropics'.

Of all the different cultural groups who arrived in the colonies in the nineteenth century, the Chinese sojourner came to stand, in the 'white' Australian mind, as the greatest threat to the nation. If the British immigrant was the exemplary newcomer and potential citizen of Australia, then the Chinese or the generic 'Asian' immigrant came to stand as the person who must be totally excluded from the nation.

Immigration restriction and enticement

From the mid-1870s the fear of Chinese migrants as potentially ruining the Australian-British 'way of life' and overrunning the continent was given voice in a variety of colonial legislation that sought to regulate arrival. From 1901 when the colonies federated, the central tool for immigration regulation was the *Immigration Restriction Act* (1901). This act (which has today become the *Migration Act*) was a wide-ranging piece of legislation that sought to regulate immigration on a number or fronts, including public health and morality, as well as on the grounds of race. The well-known contradiction is that the *Immigration Restriction Act* did not explicitly forbid immigrants from particular cultural or ethnic backgrounds from entering the nation. Rather the exclusion was implicit and policed through a 'dictation test' – a technique the Federal government picked up from its imperial brothers in southern Africa. Those who could not write in English were rejected, while 'undesirables' would be tested in another European language they did not know. So the process of making a 'white Australia' became one of repressive power (the forceful exclusion of a few individual immigrants) in tandem with self-regulation (particular migrant groups knew not to bother to apply to enter Australia).

The inception of the new Australian nation was framed in terms of a strident racialised nationalism, embodying an us-and-them mentality. Jennifer Rutherford argues that the emphatic declaration by Australian-Britons at Federation of their democratic right to protect Australia from undesirable outsiders 'provide[d] a camouflage for … an aggression directed both to an external and internal Other'.[9] The external Other was the 'coloured immigrant' or later the 'Asian hordes' who could potentially replicate the original British invasion; the internal Other were Indigenous peoples who continued to unsettle the settler through challenges to the legitimacy of 'white' belonging.

In the period from 1901 to 1939 millions of Britons were leaving their homeland. As in earlier periods, however, the vast majority went to North America. Encouraging migration to Australia again had to be a matter of enticement. The somewhat neglected policy of assisted passage for British migrants was revived and over half a million Britons moved across the oceans to Australia. As in a much earlier period the British government was keen to use emigration as a means to stabilise its domestic economy, seeking to export excess citizens. Philanthropic groups developed a number of assisted passage schemes. These included the Dreadnought Trust (the way in which a branch of this author's family made its way to Australia), Barnardo, the British Dominions Emigration Society and the Big Brother Movement. Churches were also part of developing assisted passage schemes. Despite the revived emphasis on assisted migration in the first fifty years of Federation, natural increase was the major factor in population growth. By 1947 less than 10 per cent of the population had been born overseas, and of course of those born overseas most were born in Britain.[10] It was also the period in which the White Australia policy was in full force. So the idea of Australian women giving birth to Australian babies to create a bigger and stronger nation fitted perfectly with the times.

Post-war immigration boom

By the time World War II ended in 1945 the old worries about an invasion from 'Asia' into the 'empty north' had been reinforced by the Japanese army's relentless southern march during the war. At the war's end, the rhetoric of a 'white Australia' had new purchase. The post-war years also saw an increased desire to move Australia's economic profile from an agricultural idyll to a manufacturing powerhouse. This, in tandem with the rhetoric of needing to 'fill' the country (the population was 7.3 million at this time), meant that immigration again became a central policy issue for the federal government.

In the early post-war period the government hoped to attract only 70 000 immigrants per year. However, after the devastating war in Europe there were millions of displaced persons, and the Australian government was under pressure from international organisations to accept an increased number of them. To do so would mean that the proportion of migrants of British origin would decrease. The newly appointed minister for Immigration, Arthur Calwell, was deeply committed to the new economic Australia still being a 'white Australia', famously declaring that he hoped that for every 'foreign migrant' there would be ten migrants from Britain.[11] The call went out to Britishers to migrate and make Australia their home. At the same time the government responded to the European refugee crisis. In keeping with the idea of White Australia the government requested refugees from the Baltic region – a group who were seen to be fair-skinned and fair-haired. The migration program of the late 1940s reflected the competing needs of White Australia as well as humanitarian and economic goals.

As in the past, many British people took up the offers of assisted migration. But many other migrants wanted to come to Australia who were not British and 'not white'. Nor were the displaced persons who sought refuge all the more desirable northern Europeans. As the labour needs of the booming economy continued to grow the desire for a White Australia conflicted with the need for immediate labour. In looking beyond Britain the Australian government first courted various northern European countries. Still the response was insufficient. So immigrants were accepted from southern Europe and, in later decades, the Middle East. The preference for British or 'white' migrants never disappeared, and this group was still favoured in government assistance schemes. However, in the period 1948–1957 only one third of the immigrants who came to Australia were British.[12] The major non-British groups of immigrants in the postwar period were from Yugoslavia, Greece, Malta and Italy. At one level these immigration statistics reflect the triumph of labour needs over the dream of a 'white' nation.

When the government shifted its focus to non-British migrants it targetted young single men. In many ways single men, from countries considered 'inferior' to Australia, suited the economic plans of the Australian government and business community. The single male migrants came unencumbered by family. This meant the costs for the government were kept to a minimum – for example, there were no children to school, no elderly to look after. They were also a highly mobile labour force who could be sent to remote and uncomfortable workplaces, like the Snowy Mountains or the Tasmanian highlands. And they were an eager workforce with few other options. They needed to work hard, so as to earn money quickly so they could remit money to their country, or more commonly bring their family out to Australia.

The post-war immigration program was a gigantic undertaking for such a small nation. In the period 1947–1966 the population increased by approximately five million people. In the same period the workforce increased by about one million, and well over half of these workers were born overseas. As in earlier periods of high non-white immigration, this period was marked by the ambivalent attitudes of the government and the general population. Social pride at the success of the migration venture conflicted with disquiet about the newcomers taking jobs and the changing face of Australia's streets. Though not as pronounced as in the 1880s, the fear of large numbers of single non-Anglo men arriving in the country was still an issue. Unlike the solution in the 1880s – when the vilification of Chinese men as sexual predators had reinforced the policy of exclusion – this time the government broadened its recruitment policies and encouraged the migration of single women and families through reunion. Family reunion became a significant part of the immigration program.

The philosophy behind immigration at this time was assimilation. The official logic was that migrants would come to Australia and initially they would probably have a lower standard of living, but as time passed and they assimilated, they would get better jobs, better education and more opportunities. In reality, large groups of migrants remained economically, socially and politically disadvantaged. Further, the costs of cultural assimilation – loss of language, feelings of homelessness and displacement – as well as the injustice of such a policy, became more obvious. Though governments might imagine immigration as a process where grateful impoverished families left a war-torn homeland to come to a land of milk and honey, the reality was different. There was always a significant number of immigrants who returned to their homes dissatisfied with the life offered in Australia (in the late 1960s approximately 50 000 people left Australia every year). Other immigrants stayed but became politically active, lobbying the various governments to improve services to immigrants and their families.

Post-White Australian jitters

The multicultural policies of the late 1970s and 1980s were a direct response to these economic and social problems, as both major political parties tried to woo the now significant 'ethnic' vote. Instead of presuming that migrants would be fine after a chat over the fence with kindly neighbours, this new approach to immigration emphasised that specific policies and services were required if new migrants, especially ones from non-English speaking backgrounds, were to share equally in the prosperity of the nation. Governments acknowledged that they should provide the services required by new citizens to fully participate in the nation. The idea that all citizens should be loyal did not mean that everyone needed to speak the same language, practise the same religion, eat the same food or have the same family structures. Multicultural policy also recognised that particular migrant groups were socially and economically disadvantaged, and required government assistance to achieve the equity that was promised them as Australian citizens.

In the early 1970s the Australian government pulled its troops out of the long-running war in Vietnam. Hundreds of thousands of people had been displaced by this war, in particular people from the non-Communist south of Vietnam who had supported the United States and Australia in the war. In the mid-1970s these people started arriving in Australia as refugees. Most arrived as part of Australia's refugee program developed to support people displaced by the war. Others arrived without official clearance, sailing from places such as Thailand to Australia and landing as unauthorised arrivals in the north of Australia. By the time these Indo-Chinese refugees were arriving, the last vestiges of the White Australia policy had been dismantled. There was now no mention of race or ethnicity as an issue in the legislation governing migration to Australia. The shift from assimilation to 'multiculturalism' was also under way.

However, the official change in policy was not matched throughout the community. The new wave of Asian migration to Australia in the 1970s re-ignited many of the old fears and prejudices that Anglo-Australians had exhibited in the late nineteenth century. The arrival of Vietnamese and Cambodian refugees was referred to as an 'Asian invasion'. There was extensive anti-Asian sentiment and far right-wing groups lobbied for an end to immigration from Asian countries. As with the earlier wave of migration from Asia, the Vietnamese and Cambodian refugees were represented as too different to fit into the Australian nation. Many of the same prejudices were used – their very different languages, different food, different understandings of how the world worked – to argue that these people should not be allowed to enter Australia.

By the late 1980s there was a feeling in parts of the community that the policies of multiculturalism had gone too far. Some people, especially on the political right, were arguing that migrants were receiving special treatment. They also argued that the arrival and support of migrants was dividing Australia. Over the ten years of multicultural policy there had been a proliferation of services and rights extended to new citizens. This was interpreted by some people as 'special treatment'. This disquiet was picked up by conservative politicians and used to fuel unrest.

Though the reactions to Asian immigrants in the 1970s resembled those of the 1880s, there were also many differences. What had changed in the intervening one hundred years or so was the general understanding of 'race' and racism. In 1975 the Federal government had passed the *Racial Discrimination Act*. Further, the lessons of the Holocaust showed where arguments about racial superiority could end. More specifically, by the late twentieth century the Australian government recognised and responded to issues of migrant disadvantage – especially in relation to migrants from non-English speaking backgrounds. Yet despite these differences, the representations of the new group of immigrants drew on similar tropes as those used in earlier narratives. Images tended to show the unauthorised migrants arriving by boat on the north coast of Australia, rather than the orderly arrival at Mascot (Sydney) or Tullamarine (Melbourne) airports. Popular responses in the form of graffiti exhorted: 'Asians go home'.

In the mid-1980s the historian Geoffrey Blainey ignited a debate on multiculturalism when he made comments about the pace of immigration from Asia being too fast and threatening the fabric of the Australian nation. Federal parliamentarian and future prime minister John Howard made similar comments in 1988. He said that changes in immigration policy were too rapid and that 'although the original intent of multiculturalism may have been desirable, it has gone off the rails'.[13] Similarly, in 1996 when the new political party One Nation was at the height of its popularity, and Pauline Hanson – the newly elected federal member for the party – was a central figure, many of her comments reflected a belief that particular types of immigrants were too different and destroying the Australian way of life.

What is important about these comments is that they still imagine a base for Australian culture that is British. There is still a belief in these comments that what makes Australia 'Australian' is a singular culture. These commentators and politicians see that singular culture as deriving from a time before 1945 and a set of cultural values that originate in Britain. That this belief undermines that status of millions of current Australian citizens, who were born overseas or whose family cultures are not British, is not seen as important.

In the twenty-first century the twin anxieties of invasion and difference have still not completely disappeared. They still inform much of the way in which international affairs and immigration are understood in Australia. In the early 2000s there was a spate of unauthorised arrivals on Australia's shores. These arrivals mostly came in old boats via Indonesia and sought refugee status in Australia. Many were fleeing oppressive regimes in Afghanistan and Iraq. Given the tens of thousands of unauthorised arrivals who make their way across the borders of European countries every year, the few thousand arrivals on Australia's shores was quite an insignificant trickle. However, this was not the way many Australians understood the situation. The arrival of these potential refugees was met by new government initiatives that resulted in the creation of hierarchies of being 'Australian' or being 'in Australia'. Some Australian territories – islands along the extensive north coast – were excised from the nation for the purposes of immigration. So an Australian citizen could go to Christmas Island and be in Australia, but a new and unauthorised refugee who arrived there was not considered to have reached Australian territory.

>─+◆──O──◆+─<

Immigration has shaped the Australian nation. Whether intakes of migrants were high or low, authorised or unauthorised, welcome or unwelcome, the arrival and departure of people has always been part of the project of the nation. The way in which arrivals are imagined in terms of the nation reflects Australian understanding of home and belonging. Although Australia today is one of the most multicultural nations on earth, and although government immigration policies are now open to all, it would be remiss to forget how recent these racially non-specific and multicultural policies are. They are only 30 years old and already they are being chipped away. The Australian nation inhabits a place that has been the home of Indigenous peoples for over 40 000 years. The success of immigration and the new identities it created has often been at the expense of Indigenous peoples. It has also traditionally privileged a 'white' migrant. A just Australia will be one where the rights and voices of Indigenous people and recently arrived non-British migrants are equally privileged in the national project.

Notes

1 Sara Wills, 'Un-stitching the lips of a migrant nation', *Australian Historical Studies*, 33: 118, 2002, pp 71-89.

2 Michael Cannon, *Who's Master? Who's Man? Australia in the Victorian Age*, Sydney, 1971, p 118.

3 WD Borrie, *The European Peopling of Australasia: a demographic history 1788-1988*, Canberra, 1994, p 67.

4 C Manning Clark, *A Short History of Australia*, Victoria, 1995, p 259.

5 Borrie, *European Peopling*, p 67.

6 Jacquie Templeton, '"Italy is whoever gives us bread": migration between Lombardy and Victoria 1850-1914', in David Fitzpatrick (ed), *Home or Away: immigrants in colonial Australia*, vol 3, *Visible immigrants*, Canberra, 1992, p 42.

7 Borrie, *European Peopling*, p 145.

8 John Barnes, *The Writer in Australia: a collection of literary documents 1856-1964*, Melbourne, 1969.

9 Jennifer Rutherford, *The Gauche Intruder: Freud, Lacan and the White Australia fantasy*, Melbourne, 2000, p 10.

10 James Jupp, *Immigration*, Sydney, 1991, p 95.

11 Geoffrey Sherington, *Australia's Immigrants 1788-1978*, Sydney, 1980, p 128.

12 Sherington, *Australia's Immigrants*, p 132.

13 Stephen Castles et al, *Mistaken Identity: multiculturalism and the demise of nationalism in Australia*, Sydney, 1992, pp 171-72.

CHAPTER SEVEN

SYMBOLS OF AUSTRALIA

Richard White

In 1999 Australians voted against becoming a republic. At the same time, they voted on a new preamble to their Constitution which attempted to put into words what the nation stood for: mostly conventional sentiments celebrating unity, diversity, freedom, tolerance, independence, equality and so on. The tortuous drafting of an acceptable form of words was overshadowed by the republic debate, but it generated considerable disagreement and some mockery, particularly about the Australianism 'mateship', about whether God should be present and the appropriate description of prior Aboriginal relations to the land ('ownership', 'custodianship', 'kinship' or mere 'occupation'). The preamble was rejected by an even larger majority than was the republic.

While it is not surprising that a community has trouble agreeing on the values it shares, the fate of the preamble stands in stark contrast to what seemed to be wide public approval of another attempt to represent the nation: the spectacle of the opening ceremony for the Sydney Olympics the following year. There, it seemed, 'before the eyes of the world', Australians had no difficulty finding their identity in a host of symbols – flags, native animals, stockmen from the 'bush', the suburban paraphernalia of lawnmowers and Hills Hoist clotheslines – jostling together to represent them.

The contrast is instructive – but what exactly is the lesson? That words are inevitably more controversial than visual symbols in representing the nation? That the surprise element – the opening was a symbolic *fait accompli* – stymied criticism whereas a long process of public debate only incited it? That the pluralism of the New South Wales state Labor government responsible for the Olympics was more in tune with public sentiment than the more unitary identity pursued by the (conservative) Liberal federal government in the pre-amble? That national identity is clearer and more coherent before an international audience than in a discussion among Australians?

This chapter surveys a range of Australian national symbols and their bumpy careers over two centuries – a kind of tourist guide to Australia's symbolic history. In the process it addresses the intriguing questions that national symbols pose and the lessons they teach: where do they come from, what do they mean and what effect do they have?

>→·◆›·○·‹◆··◄

National symbols perform a range of different functions in contemporary society – they include and exclude, they tap emotions as well as consumer markets, they help us remember and forget, they represent nations to each other as well as to themselves. Their role is further complicated by the fact that their origins, meaning and impact have changed over the last two centuries. On the one hand, the role of the nation-state is in decline, challenged internally by other identities and externally by the process of globalisation. On the other hand, globalisation, along with the remarkable growth in our capacity to reproduce visual images since the nineteenth century, has meant competing national symbols have proliferated as never before. Once meetings of nation-states were rare outside war, tourism and sport, but now such meetings penetrate everyday life as we consume, communicate and take political action.

Australia offers a useful case-study of the invention of symbolic traditions, as a settler society only since 1788, a nation state only since 1901, a society constantly renovated by the arrival of new migrants yet still unreconciled with its Indigenous members. My emphasis here is necessarily on non-Aboriginal symbol-making: the rich symbolic languages of Aboriginal people were not conceived as 'national' symbols, though their appropriation and appreciation in the process of nation-making became an essential part of the story.

The classic national symbols are those formal symbols of state that receive some form of legitimation by government, and it is reasonable to assume that they operate differently from more popular symbols that appear to emerge more spontaneously. Flags, coats-of-arms, seals and anthems are conceived as singular and permanent; the symbols that appear on coinage and postage stamps have more scope to represent a range of changing national concerns. When the Commonwealth of Australia came into existence in 1901, it was not by revolution but by an Act of the British parliament. In *Lion and Kangaroo* (1976), Gavin Souter has shown how the new government sought a bipartisan if banal consensus in producing symbols to represent the new nation. Contrived to reflect the constitutional reality – a nation state within the British Empire – they also probably satisfied the dual loyalties that most Australians, when they thought about it, had to Britain and Australia: a complex mix of racism, imperial sentiment and local patriotic feeling summed up in the description of the new citizenry as 'independent Australian Britons'.[1]

Official symbols tended to combine relatively neutral symbols of Australia – the Southern Cross, and Australian flora and fauna – with symbols of the British connection, such as the Union Jack, the Cross of Saint George, the lion and the crown. Most had their critics. The history of the Australian flag demonstrates how a symbol can be seen as partisan by some, but for others can acquire a naturalness through familiarity, and can convey new meanings to both supporters and opponents as time goes on. The result of a competition with restrictive guidelines, the Australian flag combined the Union Jack with the Southern Cross, and a six-pointed 'Commonwealth' star representing the six colonies that were uniting, now as states, to form the nation.[2]

The flag was not formally legislated until the *Flags Act* of 1953, when it was established that the Australian flag *alone* represented Australia.

From the 1960s – stimulated in part by Canada's adoption for its centenary of what was widely seen in Australia as a modern and attractive new flag – there was increasing debate about the flag, which predictably erupted each Australia Day. On the one hand the feeling for the Australian flag gained increasing intensity as it lost its novelty and represented a greater quantum of shared experience. In particular the fact that Australia has 'gone to war' under the flag was seen in some circles, particularly the Returned Serviceman's League, to give it particular emotional value. On the other hand the presence of the Union Jack on the Australian flag was seen as increasingly irrelevant to a population which was drawn less and less from Britain after World War II. As the British relationship declined and as Britain withdrew west of Suez and into Europe, republican sentiment gained currency. Proposals for a new Australian flag were drawn up on a regular basis, and from 1981, Ausflag – a private non-profit organisation – stimulated debate and ran flag competitions. In the many and varied proposals, the Southern Cross remains the most popular symbol. But in 2004, in the lead-up to an election, Prime Minister John Howard could still see political gain in forcing schools to fly the national flag, seeking to deflect criticism that his government had surrendered Australian sovereignty to the United States in the second Iraq war and the Free Trade Agreement. At the same time there were complaints that, for rugby games between Australia and New Zealand, the flags are almost indistinguishable: they reminded at least one commentator of Jerry Seinfeld's quip, 'I love your flag. Britain at night …'[3]

Other formal symbols proved less controversial, but still attracted mild derision. The Australian coat-of-arms, granted in 1912 (replacing an earlier 1908 form), made use of the kangaroo and emu, the Commonwealth star and the wattle blossom, as well as the emblems of the six states which incorporated British symbols. Coinage commonly used native animals on the reverse (the monarch's bust was on the obverse), but have also used symbols of produce (ears of wheat, the ram's head) and busts of Aborigines. The decimalisation of the Australian currency in 1966 provided the opportunity for a complete re-design of the coinage, which stuck with animals and the monarchy. Postage stamps have increasingly widened their range of subjects from these basic symbols – which survived through the first half of the twentieth century – to a multiplicity of subjects most of which could not be thought of as national symbols.

None of these symbols was simply imposed by the state; but nor were they the volcanic effusions of deep-seated national consciousness. In the historiography of Federation in Australia there has been a dramatic shift, coinciding with the lead-up to the Centenary of Federation in 2001. When Australian history emerged from the universities in the 1960s, often influenced by a radical nationalist tradition, the federation movement was commonly seen, even mocked, as a somewhat cynical process; an imposition of a political elite on an indifferent population. (Analysing the ballots, it is possible to make the debating point that only 11.5% of the population voted in favour of federation.[4]) But a later generation of historians has taken a more favourable view of the nation-making process, presenting Federation as a popular movement. Helen Irving, Bob Birrell and John Hirst have argued for the existence of – in Hirst's phrase – a 'sentimental nation' that pre-dated the formal establishment of a nation state; a national feeling that had a more organic relation to 'the people'.[5] Certainly the formal symbols of state drew on a well-established and widely accepted symbolic language. And just as certainly, national symbols, both formal and informal, depend for their effectiveness on their apparent natural emergence from an agreed, organic national identity. The questions remain as to whether their appearance was organic or imposed, the expression of sentiment or invention of tradition; and what purchase they might have had on the general population, manufacturing a banal nationalism, summing up widely held sentiment – or in fact not having much effect at all.

Clearly the formal symbols of the new nation-state were not

manufactured out of thin air. Well before Federation, there were many alternative symbolic languages, official and unofficial, jostling to represent this new, nebulous thing that people were calling Australia. Each colony had its own formal symbols of state, usually combining colonial and British emblems. But Australians were using a range of symbols in a range of less official contexts, from home decoration to trade-marks to cartoons, to express their colonial identity pictorially. Significantly, in this vernacular use of symbols there was usually no overt reference to the British connection, no need felt to balance a statement of colonial difference with an assurance of continued imperial loyalty.

In the designing of flags and emblems, the preference was for the language of the heavens – the Southern Cross and the rising sun. The Southern Cross appeared on flags from the early 1820s. Most famously it starred on the flag raised at the Eureka Stockade near Ballarat (Victoria) in 1854, when an organised resistance grew among immigrants attracted by the discovery of gold in 1851. They opposed what they saw as an autocratic and inept colonial government. When troops attacked their primitive stockade, the diggers were easily defeated. The meaning of that skirmish – one of the few bloody conflicts on Australian soil that was not part of the dispossession of Indigenous Australians – has been a favourite debating point in Australian history. Were the 'diggers', a cosmopolitan mix of predominantly middle-class adventurers, fighting the cause of liberty; or Irish nationalism; or their rights as Englishmen; or tax avoidance; or even multiculturalism? Whatever the cause, they fought under their own flag. Rafaello Carboni, who had been active in the Young Italy movement, gave a first-hand account of the uprising in *The Eureka Stockade* (Melbourne, 1855), and wrote of the Eureka flag: 'There is no flag in Europe or in the civilised world half so beautiful ... but all exceedingly chaste and natural'. Its meaning has remained fluid enough for a surprising range of interests to lay claim to it, from the Catholic Church, the Communist Party of Australia and neo-Nazis to the Builders Labourers' Federation and motorbike gangs.

The rising sun was another popular 'natural' symbol by Federation. It had the advantage of identifying the newly emerging Australia with the future, distinguishing it from the preoccupation with the past in the symbolism of many older nations. It appeared on the New South Wales and South Australian coats of arms. It was a common decorative device, particularly in the style of architecture, retrospectively known as 'Federation', which was popular at the turn of the century.[6] The rising sun would often feature as decoration on the main gable. On Australia House in London – assertively facing east – the sun motif was represented by Apollo in a dramatic sculpture. The badge designed for the Australian military forces in 1902 became commonly known as the rising sun, and the Australian defence forces commonly identified with it. However, the connection with the flag of Japan, Australia's main enemy in World War II, saw the rising sun fall into disrepute as an Australian symbol. Fifty years on there has been a campaign to revive it.

Distinctive fauna also provided popular national symbols from an early date. The kangaroo has been the most enduring and widely recognised of all Australian national symbols, but the emu, the lyrebird, the koala, the platypus and the kookaburra have also had their moments. The development of a self-consciously Australian cuisine from the 1980s encouraging the use of kangaroo meat led to some debates about whether or not national symbols ought to be eaten.

Australian marsupials, so very peculiar in the eyes of the rest of the world, were perhaps obvious sources of distinctive symbols. Australian flora needed more work, yet from the 1880s wildflowers formed the basis of a developing Australian school of design: art nouveau motifs based on the waratah, wattle, bottlebrush and eucalyptus were particularly popular. Interestingly, the most significant figures in this quite self-conscious production of national symbols were three migrants who left Europe in their twenties: the remarkable Lucien Henry, communard artist transported to New Caledonia in 1872 who then became lecturer in Art at the Sydney Technical College; JH Maiden, London-trained botanist and director of

Sydney's Botanic Gardens; and RT Baker, another English migrant who became director of the Museum of Applied Arts and Sciences (the Powerhouse Museum) in Sydney. Partly through their international perspective on Australian nature, they became ardent promoters of Australian flora. Building on the symbiotic relationship between botany and art, they encouraged the self-conscious admiration of Australian flora as a means of promoting national sentiment and patriotic citizenship in their adopted country.

Maiden and Baker were the leading protagonists in Australia's 'war of the roses' – the battle between advocates of the wattle and the waratah over which should be Australia's national floral symbol. The wattle won. While not as distinctively Australian as the waratah – acacias were native to other parts of the world – it was more 'national' because it was found throughout Australia, and some variety is in bloom somewhere in Australia every day of the year. The waratah was only found in three states and while it had more design possibilities, it was too cumbersome to wear in a buttonhole. The wattle also conjured up associations with purity, innocence, wholesomeness and cheerfulness, values which were vigorously promoted as representative of white Australia; the fleshy voluptuousness of the waratah suggested an almost old-world decadence.[7]

The promotion of flora and fauna as national symbols stimulated a conservationist ethic among many Australians which ran counter to a tradition of developmentalism and exploitation, although the zeal with which wildflower enthusiasts rampaged through the bush gathering armfuls of flowers to decorate their homes possibly did more environmental harm than good. The symbolic role of plants has reflected on gardening practices so that at different times the planting of native gardens has been seen as a nationalist act. With the development of cultivars, native plants have been thoroughly commodified. Western Australian natives particularly have colonised the suburban gardens of the eastern states. The devotion to the symbolic or simply decorative possibilities of flowers and gum leaves continued into the arts and crafts movement of the 1900s, in the art deco of the 1920s, in the revived crafts movement of the 1970s and the up-market tourist fashions of the 1990s.[8]

The symbolic languages of flowers, of animals, and of the heavens were seen as relatively neutral, but they were not value-free. Originally they reflected the Enlightenment's scientific interest in astronomy and natural history – a European view of what was distinctive about Australia. Their acceptance as national symbols by the Australian-born was part of a colonial habit of deference and self-definition with an eye to how others see Australians.[9] So the kangaroo was considered representative of Australia because it was a scientific oddity in European eyes; whereas the British lion, the Welsh dragon, the American eagle or the Danish elephant were chosen as symbols of national strength.

Other symbols in the nineteenth century moved beyond natural phenomena, and their underlying political meaning is more overt. One was the classical convention of an idealised woman, an Australian equivalent of Britannia, Columbia or Marianne. Usually blonde, befitting the land of the wattle, and often carrying a crook representing the wool industry, she was always young, clear-eyed and innocent. In cartoons she was often depicted as vulnerable to foreign threats, or as the daughter of John Bull, with an implied balance between a continuing filial duty to Britain and the growing need to assert her independence. An alternative figure representing many of the same values was the 'little boy from Manly' (a Sydney beach suburb), who first appeared in *Bulletin* cartoons in 1885, after a Sydney youngster had generously donated the contents of his money box to the Sudan War fund. He brought (a somewhat juvenile) masculinity and greater assertiveness - even impetuosity – to national symbolism.[10] However, both figures fell into disuse after World War I.

Just as value-laden was the use of particular products, as particular sectors of the economy competed for a symbolic place at the heart of the nation. The golden fleece, the miner's pick or the stook of wheat were common, often grouped together equating the nation with its economic resources. A more general pastoral image of sheep and gum trees was popularised by the Heidelberg School, a group of artists intent on creating a national style. Theirs became the most widely accepted summation of the 'real' Australia by the end of the nineteenth century, despite the fact that Australia was highly urbanised. In general it might be said that the imagined landscape, rather than the imagined community, and the 'bush' rather than the city, have supplied the majority of Australia's national symbols – though Graeme Davison has noted the symbolic power of the rapidly growing Australian city in the 1880s.[11]

More complex was the use of certain occupations – the miner, stockman or shearer – to represent the nation. Russel Ward has shown how this 'nomad tribe' of bush workers, particularly those involved in the wool industry, became powerful symbols of a more radical Australian nationalism and were widely seen as representing the 'typical' Australian. They were often depicted, in the *Bulletin* for example, in direct opposition to British interests. Yet what gave the male bush worker his ultimate legitimacy as a national symbol was the role he played in the imperial economy, and increasingly in the empire's wars. Again it was often English visitors who identified him as a distinctive character; Francis Adams famously identified the 'bushman' as 'The one powerful and unique type yet produced in Australia'.[12] He was respectable enough to represent democratic Australia at Queen Victoria's jubilee, and to lead the Federation procession in 1901.

At a time when war was seen as the conclusive test of a nation's worth, citizen soldiers were thought to represent the nation's fitness not just symbolically but in actual life – and death. The enthusiastic and traumatic involvement of Australians in 'the Great War', popularly represented as the new nation's entry onto the world stage, produced its own set of emotionally charged symbols and rituals. The popular image of the World War I 'digger' (or Anzac) celebrated anti-authoritarianism, drinking sprees and 'larrikinism' – the loutish culture of urban ruffians. But as a national symbol, the digger was ennobled to stand for the conventional masculine virtues of the day.

Ken Inglis and Graham Seal have examined in detail the complex symbolic language and role of the many war memorials that sprang up after World War I, which, with the war dead buried on the other side of the world, were required to take on the role of a surrogate graveside.[13] The functional ambiguity of that symbolic language proved itself in memorials which could simultaneously celebrate national military prowess, testify to the waste of war and assuage painful personal loss. Legislation banning the commercial exploitation of 'Anzac' and related words placed the digger's symbolic role in spiritually representing the nation above all other symbols. No other national symbol had the same protection from commercial exploitation until 1988, when words related to the Bicentenary received similar legislative protection. (In that case however, it was to allow for their more effective commercial exploitation when rights to their use were sold to sponsors.)

Which brings us to the commercial use of national symbols. Legislative protection for 'Anzac' was acknowledgment that national symbols were exploited mercilessly with the development of packaging, illustrated advertising, brand names, trade marks and a mass consumer economy from the late nineteenth century. Around the turn of the century it was possible to buy Boomerang sheet music, Kangaroo bicycles, Koala quilts, Possum wines and Cooee cigarettes.[14] They worked not only to appeal to national sentiment, but to map the Australian domestic market, particularly against imports from overseas. Their role in this symbolic definition of Australia as a market was arguably a far more potent force in the creation of national sentiment, in that they penetrated further into homes and into everyday life than more formal symbols of state. But clearly while they were being imposed on the market-place, they could only be successful as marketing strategies if the public accepted them as symbols they could identify with. Perhaps it is significant that many of those trade marks failed to survive.

Those that did survive provided some of the most powerful national symbols – Billy tea, Rosella tomato sauce, the Qantas kangaroo. With the expansion of the heavy industrial base from the 1920s, the bias towards rural symbolism was challenged by the city. The surf lifesaver, integral to the new beach culture that appeared in Australia in the 1900s, became a popular national symbol between the wars: he combined the bushman's mateship and the Anzac's brave sacrifice in a more urban context.[15] The Sydney Harbour Bridge, completed in 1932, symbolised industrial progress, while the Sydney Opera House, opened in 1972, became a readily recognisable symbol of urban sophistication. The beach itself, particularly Bondi in Sydney, was associated nationally and internationally with an image of the 'sun-bronzed Aussie' and a love of sun and leisure. With increased international tourism, what was being packaged and marketed was Australian culture itself. By 2004 the totality of tourist symbols was being marketed by government as Brand Australia.

National symbols were further commercialised with the advent of television in 1956 and the increasing sophistication of advertisers in the manipulation of images. By the 1980s, as new products developed national markets (beer, sport and media particularly), and the relative importance of Australian manufacturing in the domestic market declined, there was a revival of outback imagery. The successful 1983 America's Cup challenge used a boxing kangaroo; 'Crocodile Dundee' revived a conservative version of the bushman; and Uluru (Ayers Rock) came to symbolise the heart of Australia. A 1990s advertising campaign for the Australian petrol company Ampol, which featured a bush worker astride a motorbike, dressed in a drizabone and holding a cattle dog under the slogan 'I'm as Australian as Ampol', was perhaps the cleverest, and most cynical, attempt to position a commercial interest in the marketplace through the appropriation of national symbols: the brand itself becomes the test of national loyalty. At the same time, one of the most active exploiters of national symbolism was (and is) McDonald's hamburger chain. Most of those 'iconic' brand names are now owned by foreign corporations but that has not affected their ability to use a nationally accepted symbolic language to position themselves in the market.

While national symbols proliferated commercially, formal attempts to develop national symbolism appropriate to a consciously multicultural nation foundered. We have seen no widely agreed alternative to the national flag: too many, perhaps, look like tawdry company logos. Neither the Bicentennial nor the Centenary of Federation produced effective new symbols. The search for a mascot for the 2000 Olympic Games inevitably returned to the traditional fauna, but the decision to go for not one but three indicated not just the difficulty of plumping for one, but the greater opportunities for commercial exploitation. A new parliament house and the National Museum of Australia each developed elaborate symbolic forms in such a way that their meaning needed equally elaborate explanation. The latter's use of what has become an interesting new symbol – the word 'Eternity' in copperplate handwriting broken into indecipherable squiggles for decorative purposes – would seem especially arcane. This recent addition to Australia's symbolic repertoire recalls Arthur Stace who, following a religious conversion in the 1930s, spent his days chalking the word 'Eternity' on the streets of Sydney. The artist Martin Sharp employed it, and it was the focus of the Millennium New Year's Eve fireworks spectacle on Sydney's Harbour Bridge. But what symbolic meaning is it supposed to convey:- Sydney's urban sophistication, nostalgia for past eccentricity, vague spiritual awareness, a New Age take on an Aboriginal Dreamtime? The only certainty is that Arthur Stace's own meaning, a fire and brimstone warning, is irrelevant.

While native plants and animals supplied a constant stream of national symbolism, the possibilities of Aboriginal culture were largely ignored, perhaps because white nationality was built on the dispossession of Indigenous people. When Aboriginal figures were used in trade marks before World War I, it was usually in a humorous and derogatory context. However this was not always the case with Aboriginal symbols. The boomerang and the 'Cooee' have a more complex history, as have some formal symbols from the nineteenth century – Sydney's coat of arms, an early South Australian flag – depicting the meeting of the two cultures.[16] The craft movement between the wars showed increasing interest in Aboriginal motifs, and in the 1950s Aboriginal figures and artefacts provided popular ornaments, garden statuary, souvenirs and national decoration – for example in the Commonwealth jubilee in 1951, and souvenirs of the Queen's visit in 1954. Boomerangs particularly were commonly accepted as a symbol of Australia, dominating the souvenir market but also, for example, in the Buy Australian campaign launched in 1961.

From the 1980s the appropriation of Aboriginal symbols as Australian national symbols increased. They are often called on to fill a symbolic vacuum left by the breaking of monarchical ties, and are often seen as providing a spiritual dimension otherwise lacking in national imagery. The development of the tourist industry, a new international market for Aboriginal art and the symbolic handover of Uluru to its traditional owners in 1985 are some signs of the new field. The shift to the 'red centre' of Australia as the symbolic heart was also evident in the (intentionally) understated symbolism of the new parliament house and the National Museum. The Aboriginal flag, designed by Harold Thomas in 1971, has found a wide acceptance in the non-Aboriginal community and is often suggested as a symbolic element in any new national flag. The increasing recognition of the vibrancy and sophistication of Aboriginal culture has opened up a whole new quarry of national symbolism. The motives for this movement are ambiguous and not easy to unpick however: they range from reconciliation and sincere imitation, to appropriation, absorption by the dominant culture, and the desire for the approbation of – and commercial advantage in – the outside world.[17]

>─┼─◆>─0─<◆─┼─<

What tentative conclusions can we reach from all this about the three questions raised at the outset: where have these symbols come from, what have they meant, and what effect have they had? In terms of origins, two points might be made. As in understandings of the origin of the nation itself, explanations of the origin of national symbols might be said to swing between their being the spontaneous expression of popular feeling and the imposition or 'invention' of dominant groups. While this brief survey might suggest neither explanation is adequate in any simple way, the complex interaction of sectional interests, political power and popular response is interesting.

Secondly, it becomes apparent how often national symbols were created, reproduced and popularised in contexts that encouraged transnational comparisons (particularly imperial ones). International sport, war, trade and tourism are obvious stimuli to the production of national symbols, but it is also worth noting how symbols are caught in more delicate transnational webs: the role of migrants in promoting distinctive flora, an awareness of an international gaze in the move away from overtly racial symbols, and the international impulse to standardise symbols of national difference. Identity can only ever be defined against the other.

As to what symbols might mean, they seem to be infinitely permeable, any one symbol meaning all things to all people as detached meanings flow in and out and through the graphic image. Indeed the ambiguity of meaning is essential to the success of a symbol in obscuring dissension and diversity within a community. The rising sun could simultaneously represent both the imperial ambitions of a new nation as Australia's rays shone (somewhat illogically) over the south Pacific and a utopian vision of a future socialist paradise. Anzac memorials could simultaneously stand for militarism and mourning, for larrikinism and nobility, for duty and anti-authoritarianism.

In that case the function of a national symbol lies not in its capacity to convey particular shared meanings, but in its power to spark recognition in a population in which shared understanding of what the nation stands for is impossible. Its role is thus to identify and map, to imagine the community without imagining it united. One of the most powerful ways of imagining a community is to imagine it as a market. Of all individuals, those who imagine the nation as a market have most to gain. It is no coincidence that the nineteenth-century formation of nation states emerged in tandem with mass national markets – as distinct from the earlier consumerism of transnational elites. The nation provided not just a market for goods, but a market for ideas – politicians, writers, academics also imagined markets, spheres of action, audiences for their operations, most often national. In that situation it is not necessary that the symbols convey meaning: indeed their function is best served when they remain ambiguous.

The final question to ask is what impact national symbols might have. Michael Billig and Tim Edensor have argued for the over-whelming penetration of the nation's symbolic power into the mundane and everyday, 'the quotidian realms experienced most of the time by most people'.[18] We can see how greater globalisation, greater 'mediatisation' and increased availability of images have made national symbols inescapable, saturating everyday life as never before. Yet we also need to recognise the considerable limits to that process. The greater reflexivity and self-consciousness of modern life places one such limit as individuals distance themselves from national symbols. In a number of instances attempts to popularise Australian symbols have met with mockery, particularly whenever more formal, state-sanctioned proposals for symbols are debated, from Federation to its centenary. The mockery itself waxes and wanes: at different times Aboriginal Australians and Anzacs have been subjected to public ridicule – but they are not so today – whereas Captain Cook or a British racial heritage are now open to mockery when once they commanded more respect. In addition many symbols have been con-tested, some vigorously, others more by neglect or by the substitu-tion of alternatives. The sheer impossibility of creating a shared symbolic language is more widely recognised, as is the (perhaps post-modern) consciousness of the plurality of meaning. Singular national narratives have been challenged by late twentieth-century 'History Wars', particularly coinciding with the emergence of a powerful Indigenous critique of conventionally celebratory histories of European settlement in Australia, with 'multicultural' politics and with the women's movement.

However, these more self-conscious rejections of national symbols, as suggestive as they are, do not answer the argument as to how 'second nature' national identities have arisen through the proliferation of banal national symbols. Indeed Edensor might argue that that very mockery is second nature to an Australian national character. But deducing the nation where there is no self-consciousness of it is a risky business. There are moments when individuals perform a banal nationalism: ordinary people do enact the nation, when processing a visa application, watching the Olympics or buying Vegemite in London. But we should also recognise that most people most of the time are not performing nationality; mostly people act as people, outside the media circus, outside transnational comparisons. It is likely that academics, caught in mundanely national webs of significance more than most, are inclined to overstate the power of nation and of national symbols. And that might leave some room for hope.

Notes

1   Keith Hancock, *Australia*, London, 1930; NK Meaney, 'Britishness and Australian identity: the problem of nationalism in Australian history and historiography', *Australian Historical Studies* 32: 116, 2001, pp 76-90.

2   Elizabeth Kwan, 'Australian flag: ambiguous symbol of nationality in Melbourne and Sydney, 1920-21', *Australian Historical Studies*, 26:103, 1994, pp 280-303; Carol A Foley, *The Australian Flag: colonial relic or contemporary icon?*, Sydney, 1996.

3   'The Fitz files', *Sydney Morning Herald*, 14 August 2004, p 77.

4   Peter Botsman, *The Great Constitutional Swindle: a citizen's view of the Australian constitution*, Sydney, 2000, p 52.

5   Helen Irving, *To Constitute a Nation: a cultural history of Australia's constitution*, Cambridge, 1997; John Hirst, *The Sentimental Nation: the making of the Australian Commonwealth*, Melbourne, 2000; Bob Birrell, *Federation: the secret story*, Sydney, 2001.

6   Trevor Howells and Michael Nicholson, *Towards the Dawn: federation architecture in Australia 1890-1915*, Sydney, 1989.

7   Ann Stephen (ed), *Visions of a Republic: the work of Lucien Henry - Paris - Noumea - Sydney*, Sydney, 2001; Maria Hitchcock, *Wattle*, Canberra, 1991;

Libby Robin, 'Nationalising nature: Wattle Days in Australia', *Journal of Australian Studies*, 73, 2002, pp 13-26.

8 Grace Cochrane, *The Crafts Movement in Australia: a history*, Sydney, 1992.

9 Richard White, 'The outsider's gaze and the representation of Australia' in Don Grant and Graham Seal (eds), *Australia in the World: perceptions and possibilities*, Perth, 1994, pp 22-28.

10 Robert Crawford, 'A slow coming of age: advertising and the Little Boy from Manly in the twentieth century' *Journal of Australian Studies*, 67, 2001, pp 126-43.

11 Graeme Davison, *The Rise and Fall of Marvellous Melbourne*, Melbourne, 1978.

12 Francis Adams, *The Australians*, London, 1893, p165.

13 KS Inglis, *Sacred Places: war memorials in the Australian landscape*, Melbourne, 1998; Graham Seal, *Inventing ANZAC: the digger and national mythology*, Brisbane, 2004.

14 Mimmo Cozzolino, *Symbols of Australia*, Melbourne, 1980.

15 Kay Saunders, '"Specimens of superb manhood": the lifesaver as national icon', *Journal of Australian Studies*, 56, 1998, pp 96-105.

16 Richard White, 'Cooees across the Strand: Australian travellers in London and the performance of national identity', *Australian Historical Studies*, 32:116, 2001, pp 109-27.

17 Jan Kociumbas, 'Performances: indigenisation and postcolonial culture', in Hsu-Ming Teo and Richard White (eds), *Cultural History in Australia*, Sydney, 2003, pp 127-41.

18 Michael Billig, *Banal Nationalism*, London, 1995; Tim Edensor, *National Identity, Popular Culture and Everyday Life*, Oxford, 2002, p 17.

CHAPTER EIGHT

AUSTRALIANS AND WAR

Melanie Oppenheimer and Bruce Scates

At the centre of almost every Australian city and town stands a war memorial. Obelisk and arch, broken pillar and stern upright soldier, these gestures of remembrance mark Australia's physical and cultural landscape. Most of them bear the name of Anzac, the acronym for the Australian and New Zealand Army Corps. Now a popular byword for all Australian servicemen and women, 'Anzac' commemorated Australia's first costly military engagement as a nation on the beaches and gullies of the Gallipoli peninsula in Turkey in 1915. Sydney's Anzac Memorial lies in Hyde Park; a quiet place in the midst of a busy city; solid, sombre but somehow reassuring. It is difficult to imagine the memorial as a site of much controversy. But it was.

A memorial had been mooted from the early days of Australia's involvement in the Great War, but few could agree on its position or its purpose. Many in the New South Wales government favoured some form of edifice at the southerly approach to the Sydney Harbour Bridge; the style would be grand, triumphant and certain to match any shrine they might build down in Melbourne (Sydney's long-time rival). Grieving parents were not so provincial. For them the wharves at Woolloomooloo in eastern Sydney had long been a site of pilgrimage; there they had said goodbye to sons lost in a war a world away. Then there were those deeply troubled by the politics of remembrance. By the 1920s, as most of Australia's war memorials were built, conservatives warned of a corrosive 'disloyal element'; pacifists who opposed the 'militarisation' of parks and playgrounds with captured artillery; feminists, anti-conscriptionists and Bolsheviks whose internationalism was at once 'unBritish', 'unAustralian', and 'unAnzac'.

In the end, the politics of Sydney's Anzac Memorial were intensely gendered. The architect, Bruce Dellit, believed war memorials, by definition, were a tribute to men: '[They] must be strong, original and essentially masculine, for ... the conflict was mainly the concern of men'. But the contribution of women was not so easily marginalised. Many of the monument's sculptures depict nurses ministering to the fallen; they are symbols of life and compassion in a battlefield brimming with suffering and death. Women also stand at the very centre of the memorial. Three female figures – mother, sister and wife - carry the limp, naked body of a slaughtered soldier. They are his 'best beloved', their grim mourning faces steeled against their loss. Raynor Hoff, a sculptor who had 'seen too much of war to glorify it', called it the 'spirit' of women's sacrifice:

> Thousands of women ... lost all that was dearest to them – sons they had born[e] and reared, husbands, fathers of their children, friends and lovers. There was no acknowledgment of them in casualty lists of wounded, maimed and killed ... In this spirit I have shown them, carrying their load, the sacrifice of their menfolk.[1]

To shift the focus of a national war memorial away from the suffering of men and towards that of women was controversial enough. Even more alarming was Hoff's proposal for a second group-sculpture beneath the great windows of the exterior. 'The Crucifixion of Civilisation' depicted the massive figure of a naked woman, stretched over the cross-like hilt of the sword of war. Dead soldiers and debris were heaped at her feet. The proposal caused uproar. Bishops and politicians denounced it as 'blasphemous', and 'improper'. Brigadier General MacKay was not sure what 'a good piece of art' might look like but this was enough to shock the most battle-hardened soldier. The controversial sculpture was never completed.[2]

The debates surrounding Sydney's war memorial were echoed across the country. As communities struggled to come to terms with the enormity of their loss, the way they chose to remember their dead were various, complex and contested. To this day, the monuments they raised are active sites of memory, their many elusive meanings 'open to interrogation and interpretation'.[3]

Like Hoff's slaughtered soldier, Australia's loss in war weighed heavily on a young nation. In all, some 100 000 Australians have died in conflicts overseas, in battlefields scattered across Europe and Asia. Their bodies remain there. The most obvious explanation for the number, scale and enduring significance of Australia's war memorials is that they act as surrogate graves, focal points of longing and remembrance. Most of these memorials, including the one in Hyde Park, were raised to remember the dead of the Great War. In proportion to their population, it was Australia and New Zealand, Britain's most distant dominions, which lost more men than any other combatant nation (and, by the same token, built more memorials to their memory). With World War II and later conflicts, memorials became sites of multiple commemorations. New lists of names were carved in stone or cast in metal, with one generation of dead quietly joining another. Smaller memorials made necessary economies: some plaques squeeze 'Korea' 'Vietnam' or (most ominously) 'Subsequent Conflicts' around their pedestal.

Each of these conflicts had a different impact on Australian society. The first task of this chapter is to chart the changing course of Australia's involvement in war, where Australians have fought and why. This chapter will identify several different approaches to the study of war, from the traditional preoccupation with operational and tactical studies to recent forays into new fields of cultural history. The memory of war, as the debate surrounding Sydney's memorial suggests, has usually privileged the men who fought it. The final task of this chapter is to consciously shift our focus away from soldiers who shaped the 'Anzac Legend' to those other Australian who bore the burden of bereavement, and whose unpaid labour on the home front made the prosecution of war possible.

An Anzac mythology

For all the debate surrounding Sydney's memorial, the name it would take was never contentious. By the 1920s 'Anzac' had passed beyond an acronym to become a cherished and enduring cultural symbol. The reason for this (in part) is that Anzac came to symbolise so much for many different groups of people. Initially, it embodied a gesture of imperial loyalty. The landing of Australian and New Zealand troops on the Gallipoli peninsula in April 1915 was part of a British plan to force a passage through the Dardanelles and defeat the Ottoman Empire (then an ally of Germany). It was an ill-conceived, poorly resourced and hopelessly bungled exercise. The rugged landscape and a determined Turkish defence confined the Anzacs and allies to a narrow, soon-bloodstained beachhead. But by holding on at Gallipoli for eight months, a military defeat was transformed into a moral victory, a cause of both national and imperial celebration. It was at once 'Australia's baptism of fire', 'the birthplace of a nation', and proof that 'British stock' (of dubious convict antecedents for Australia at least) had not altogether degenerated in the colonies. Gallipoli may not have been Australia's most costly military involvement of the Great War but it was the first; and the very landscape of the peninsula, with its tangled gullies and plunging ravines, seemed the stuff of legends.

As the Great War progressed and as battalion after battalion was butchered on the killing fields of Europe, the meaning of Anzac steadily shifted. The resourcefulness, courage and initiative of Australian troops (or 'diggers') came to be contrasted with an incompetent, class-bound and callous British command. Anzac was invested with democratic rather than imperial traditions, the 'mateship' and egalitarianism of the trenches likened to the solidarity of trade unionism and the rough practicality of the 'bushman'. Much of this was (quite self-conscious) myth-making. The Australian Army hardly monopolised martial zeal or mateship. Its men were drawn more from the cities than the bush, and its losses on the Western Front had more to do with military structures (the number of fighting as opposed to service units) than a deliberate squandering of dominion forces. But the mythology was persuasive. CEW Bean's twelve volumes of the *Official History* added an aura of historical authenticity.[4]

Feminist historians have noted the way this 'Anzac mythology' privileged and empowered men; how soldiers in 'giving birth to a nation' laid a special (if biologically unlikely) claim to citizenship. But Anzac was always much more than a purely masculinist concept. In the wake of the war, Anzac Day (25 April) became a site for contested commemoration. While men claimed the streets in public processions, recapturing the camaraderie of war, women gathered around memorials to mourn the loved ones lost. In some cases, women's groups negotiated a place for themselves in what was largely a bastion of male privilege. The Anzac Fellowship of Women emphasised the 'sacred nature' of the day, its proximity to Easter facilitating a 'chain of remembrance'. From the end of one world war to the beginning of another, the fellowship sponsored essay-writing competitions in schools and workplaces, displacing soldier-centred stories with wider national narratives. The most powerful of these stories surrounded the legend of Private John Fitzpatrick Simpson.

A medic rather than a fighter, Private Simpson had carried wounded men to safety on the Gallipoli peninsula, aided (in a powerful biblical allusion) by a donkey. His death whilst saving others was a cogent expression of the fraternal bonds of war-time, but it was also an illustration of how the Anzac legend could be communicated to a wider audience. Compassion (and what were widely seen as female attributes of nurturing and caring) now rivalled courage and tenacity in the Anzac lexicon.[5]

The extent to which the Anzac mythology marginalised women has been widely discussed by Australian historians. There is a rich feminist historiography, led by Marilyn Lake and Joy Damousi, which has challenged and contested the memory and positioning of Anzac. The gendered nature of warfare, and position of nurses within the Anzac myth have also been debated.[6] Less discussed is the way this foundation myth served to displace Indigenous Australians.

Today, the Australian War Memorial in Canberra, the most-visited and most-revered of all Australia's museums, carefully overlooks the violence on which the nation was founded. Its colonial galleries feature displays on 'native uprisings' in the Sudan and New Zealand, China's Boxer Rebellion and the Boer War in South Africa, but Australia's own frontier wars are curiously absent.

The 'expeditionary mentality'

As the Australian War Memorial's galleries suggest, Australia's first commitment to wars overseas was as a series of colonies rather than a nation. In 1885, the New South Wales Parliament voted to send a contingent to the Sudan, to avenge the death of General Gordon at Khartoum. Expeditions to China to suppress the Boxer uprising followed. These were small-scale, poorly organised affairs, and in the case of the Sudan, the New South Wales contingent arrived too late to see much fighting.

The same could not be said of the colonial commitment to South Africa. From 1899 to 1901 (when the newly formed Commonwealth assumed responsibility for Australia's military commitment) colonies vied with one another to send men, horses and an assortment of wildlife mascots to fight Boer farmers in South Africa. In all the colonies sent some 16 000 men, of whom 600 were to die (mostly of disease) before peace was finally negotiated in 1902. They went as a demonstration of imperial loyalty – though it is debated whether enthusiasm for the war was manufactured or real, and how much these 'spontaneous' offers of troops were carefully engineered by Whitehall. The war degenerated into isolated skirmishes with Boer commandos, and a scorched-earth policy (including herding women and children into concentration camps) designed to break the will of the civilian population.[7]

While the justice of the war was always questionable, the fighting quality of Australian troops was widely acknowledged. War on the open veldt favoured the most mobile, and mounted colonial troopers were adept at living off the land and 'harassing' Boer commandos. These 'bush skills' were highly valued, and anticipated the much-vaunted qualities of the Anzac. But a far more important legacy of South Africa, and indeed all these colonial commitments, was what historians have come to call 'the expeditionary mentality'.[8]

Throughout the twentieth century, Australian troops were sent to fight in wars distant from their homeland and not always of obvious national interest to Australia. The Great War was fought to defend the British Empire. As a British dominion with no foreign policy of its own, Australia's commitment to distant battlefields in Europe and the Middle East was a foregone conclusion. The outbreak of World War II further compromised Australia's political sovereignty: in announcing hostilities in Europe in September 1939, Prime Minister Robert Menzies added that since the Empire was at war, Australia was also at war. Isolationism of any sort was simply unthinkable. As in the case of the Great War, Australian servicemen were 'surrendered' to Britain. Some 4000 Australian airmen died in Bomber command. Thousands of Australian troops were killed or captured in Greece and Crete – military fiascos driven more by politics than strategy. But by far the most costly Australian commitment was the deployment of the 8th Division to the British naval base of Singapore. When Singapore fell to the Japanese in February 1942, some 15 000 Australian troops were taken prisoner. One in three of these men was to die in captivity.[9]

With the decline of British power, Australians appeared to substitute one imperial allegiance for another. In the 1950s, Australian troops were sent to fight in Korea, a commitment to the United Nations and American alliance that cost the lives of 359 Australians. Fighting the West's cold war led to subsequent involvement in Malaya and then Indochina. Both were protracted military engagements with Australian forces unequal partners in the alliance. Vietnam alone claimed the lives of some 500 Australians (many of whom had been conscripted). Recent engagements in Afghanistan and Iraq follow a similar pattern.

Like the Anzac legend, Australia's 'expeditionary mentality' is easily exaggerated. The common argument that Australia was the victim of imperial intrigues and encumbering alliances overlooks the degree to which Australians by and large supported these military involvements. The Anzacs themselves were a volunteer force. Opposition to the Great War (and arguably even Vietnam) was driven more by domestic politics and an abhorrence of conscription than a questioning of the imperial (or for that matter the American) alliance. The 'expeditionary mentality' is also largely irrelevant to Australia's war in the Pacific from 1942–45. While recent work suggests that Japan never planned to invade Australia, there was (with the bombing of Darwin and the occupation of New Guinea) a perceived threat to Australia. In short, the assertion that Australians have died in other people's wars belies the complexity of the situation. Australia was a partner in imperial wars fought in her (real or imaginary) interest, and they were very much of Australia's own choosing.

Home fronts

Each of these overseas conflicts had a different impact on Australian society. Nineteenth-century engagements left the Australian colonies largely untouched, with relatively few casualties or long-term after effects. Australia's involvement in the Great War was a different story. It was not just the number of dead (one in five of all the 300 000 who embarked for service abroad), but with a casualty rate of 64.8 per cent, Australia became a nation of crippled soldiers. It was also a deeply divided society. For almost five years Australia mobilised not just for war overseas but also against 'the enemy within' – strikers who brought the country to a standstill in 1917, 'shirkers' who evaded military duty, imaginary German spies, and a weak but growing voice of socialist internationalism. Two divisive referenda over conscription broke the labour movement, and the Easter uprising in Ireland aroused long-standing sectarian tensions. The arrival of soldiers home only added another division – those who had seen the slaughter and those who could hardly begin to imagine it; men brutalised by battle and families unable to accept or understand them.[10]

World War II had fewer casualties than the Great War, but in many ways its effects were more far reaching. In what seemed a dramatic shift in Australian foreign policy, Prime Minister John Curtin 'put aside' previous loyalties to Great Britain and looked to the United States for 'salvation'. After the fall of Singapore in 1942, Australia became a forward base for US General Macarthur's Pacific operations. This was a total war, one that required the wholesale mobilisation of manpower and resources. Women took men's jobs 'for the duration', earning incomes and acquiring skills unthought of in peace-time. Men were conscripted to fight in New Guinea or allocated a place in essential industry. The war-time Labor government adapted surprisingly well to this quest for national efficiency.

The home front never again played such an important or enthusiastic part in the prosecution of Australia's war effort.[11] Indeed from Vietnam on, civilians at home have been spectators in Australia's wars. By far the most dramatic mobilisations against war were the Vietnam moratoriums of the late 1960s and 1970s, marches of hundreds of thousands through Australia's major cities self-consciously styled on the anti-war movement in America. War still brings Australians to the streets in protest. Mass demonstrations supported independence movements in East Timor and opposed Australia's involvement in the second Iraq war.

Writing about war

On the home front or in the firing line, covering the sharp edge of battle or its domestic implications, Australian military history has generally lacked what Joan Beaumont has called 'an integration' of these stubbornly independent fields of inquiry.[12] That is not to underestimate the achievements of Australian scholarship. For all the myth-making, CEW Bean's study of the Great War set a new standard in the canon of world military history. This was the first official history to focus more on the mentality and experience of individual soldiers than the strategies and foibles of their commanders. Bean was the forerunner of the 'face of battle' approach generally associated with the British historian John Keegan.

A focus on the experiences and emotions of individual servicemen was a legacy of Bean's tradition, though few writers have shared his obsessive love of detail.[13] Surprisingly, Bean's most ardent critics have come from the very research centre he helped to establish. Scholars based at the Australian War Memorial have struggled to redress what many see as an imbalance. Bean's Anzac mythology focused mostly on the military history of the Great War; it privileged the Army over other branches of the services, and it tested each new generation of servicemen (including today's highly trained professionals) by the increasingly archaic standards of 'the digger'. Today's military historians have a much more sobering interest in High Command: careful biographical assessments of Australia's military leaders have become their favoured historical genre.[14]

Within the academy, interest in Australia's experience of war did not really begin until the 1960s. Controversy surrounding involvement in Vietnam and the reintroduction of conscription prompted a re-evaluation of what Ken Inglis dubbed 'the Anzac tradition': the much-debated nexus between war and national identity. In the hands of feminist and social historians, more recent scholarship is less about the valour of Australian soldiers (Bean's constant refrain) than the sufferings of all victims of war. Conscientious objectors, civilian internees, conscripted Indigenous workers and bitter, broken veterans have displaced the more familiar pantheon of the Anzac.[15] Feminist scholars have explored the way war reinforces or unsettles traditional construction of gender and sexuality;[16] oral history and the careful interrogation of autobiographical narratives have unravelled the complex relationship between war's social and personal memory;[17] and cultural studies has interrogated war's representation through art, film and literature.[18] Increasingly, war is less about 'nation' than it is about communities.[19] It is a measure of the richness of Australian writings on war that it continues to open new areas of inquiry. Two such themes of this recent work have focused on the human cost of war in terms of loss, grief and mourning; and the role of unpaid civilian labour in maintaining the home front.

War and grief

Preoccupied with the role war has played in the making of national identity, historians have been slower to assess the cost of war at much more intimate levels. We have tended to assume that the grieving ended with the deaths of those it most affected. The growing number of Australians making pilgrimages to Gallipoli, Changi (the former POW camp in Malaysia), Kokoda in New Guinea, the Burma railway and the Western Front, their attempts to situate a family's and a nation's loss, and their emotional evocation of history, certainly suggest otherwise.

Joy Damousi has argued that a death in war is unlike any other. In a cruel reversal of nature, war kills the young and the able, leaving a generation of parents to mourn for their children.[20] It also destroys conventional codes of mourning. Only with the Vietnam War were the bodies of Australian soldiers brought home to their families. Before that, the bereaved lost not only loved ones, but also a body to lay to rest and a funeral to mark their passing. Perhaps worst of all though, deaths in war were essentially inconclusive. Men vanished between the beginning of one battle and the end of another, accounts of their deaths were fragmentary, inconsistent, even contradictory. In both the major wars, loss assumed a literal dimension. Bodies were swallowed in the mud, disintegrated by high explosives, condemned to the oblivion of POW camps, a limbo from which thousands would never return.

Recovering the history of grief can lead historians of war to highly personalised testimonies: diaries, letters and journals. But this is at best a selective narrative and one not altogether representative of the experience of loss and mourning. Most of the major collections were acquired in the post-war period, donated to national archives by middle-class families intent on creating a memorial to their own loved ones. Almost all address loss through the language of nationalism.

A richer, less contrived and ultimately more revealing source emerges from the chaos of war itself. In both world wars, the Australian Red Cross worked to discover the fate of missing soldiers. Their exhaustive inquiries elicit the testimony of soldiers' family and loved ones, convey the carnage of war and permit a rare insight into the 'individual ordeal' of loss and grieving. Indeed the Red Cross played the part Jay Winter has called 'fictive kin', mediating mourning for thousands of Australian families.

In these records, the voice of working-class Australians, marginalised or altogether absent in many library collections, is clear and persistent. As they relate the loss of a loved one, they often situate their grief within family and financial circumstances. It was hard enough for Mary Doherty to lose her husband in France, 'a poor fellow' who 'done his duty as well as the rest'. Harder still, was to be 'left with four children, the eldest … only 8 years and the youngest 9 months'. There was no father to love them now, no man to help them in their 'troubles': war had left her family broken and alone. The pain these correspondents express has an almost visceral quality: there is little of the pride or patriotism that so often masked the grief of middle-class testimonies. Writing from the mining town of Broken Hill, Janet Fox craved any news at all of her 'poor lad': 'He was reported missing on July 29th and I can hear nothing further you can imagine how the suspense is telling on me it seems to eat into one's very soul … how helpless I am'.[21]

These were deaths without closure. Families were angered by the 'silence' of the military authorities or outraged by all 'the inconclusive evidence … the confusion, the ambiguities, different sightings, nicknames wrong'. It was simply not enough for Mrs Jones to be told that the son she loved had 'died for his country':

I would like to know how long he lived ... did he suffer much, and was he conscious, did he ask for his parents in any way and did he send any message? I would like to know where he is buried and ... how long he was in the firing line before he was wounded. This is a dreadful war ... making so many sad homes and taking so many.[22]

Files such as these allow us a glimpse of grief at the most intimate of levels. The testimony of soldiers and loved ones (set here within the 'primary circle of mourners'[23]) bring the home front and the battle-field together. Finally, these records allow historians to witness the moment of death and bereavement; as men are machine-gunned, bayoneted or blown to pieces we feel the sharp pang of loss absent in the clichéd letters of condolence.

Unpaid labour

The memorial in Hyde Park was established in the form of a cross to allude to the important role of the Australian Red Cross during the Great War. This symbol of unpaid labour reflects a most recent theme to evolve in studies of Australians and war. Women, men and children flocked to a range of war-time charities or 'patriotic funds' as they were commonly known in Australia. These funds offered Australians a way to contribute both financially, physically and emotionally to the war effort. Volunteering gave civilians an outlet for their patriotism, their grief, their frustration and anxiety with the war. Patriotic funds were important for keeping the Australian population focused on the war effort, and were vital for maintaining soldier morale.

In the Great War, nearly A£14 million was raised across Australia for a myriad of patriotic funds, with the Australian Branch of the British Red Cross Society (as it was officially known) the largest and most important. The Australian Red Cross became an integral part of the war effort harnessing the hearts, minds, wallets and sweat of countless thousands of Australians, mainly women, who saw active participation in an international organisation as one positive way to show patriotism and support for their menfolk during the war.

The Red Cross assisted wounded and sick soldiers at home and overseas in the front line. It also helped dependents of soldiers and innocent civilians inadvertently caught up in the war in Belgium, France and elsewhere. Thousands of volunteer workers saw their work as a 'labour of love, springing with affectionate impulse from the heart of the people'.[24] Although volunteering was a popular movement, its success relied on vice-regal patronage. Lady Helen Munro Ferguson, wife of the governor-general, who founded the national organisation on the outbreak of war, was directly involved in its financial management and administration – an unusual feat for the time. The ballroom of her home, Government House in Melbourne, was transformed into a bustling factory and warehouse where Red Cross goods were created and packed by hundreds of volunteers for shipment overseas to Egypt, Britain and France.[25]

The Australian home front was activated by knitting socks, making and mending pyjamas and shirts, packing parcels, writing letters, serving, fetching and carrying countless cups of tea, cleaning wards, collecting and disposing bedpans, selling home-made produce at stalls and fetes, and generally rolling up one's sleeves and pitching in. Through the creation of these 'comforts', volunteers nurtured the body of soldiers in war; volunteer work clothed the body; fed it; nursed it; massaged it; and cared for it. Through these acts, women at home could hope to salvage and protect their menfolk from the battle scars of war on the other side of the world.

World War II replicated and extended this pattern of home front civilian volunteering. From the Australian Red Cross, with hundreds of thousands of members, to the Wallacia Comforts Club formed in western Sydney, the scope of the patriotic funds was only limited by the imagination of the people. A regular ritual throughout the war was to send parcels to loved ones on active service. The Wallacia Comforts Club was particularly inventive. It sent fruitcakes to 48 local servicemen and women using a bricklayer's cement mixer to mix the ingredients. The 48 fruitcakes were then transported to the local bakery in an old pram where they were baked free of charge, before being carefully wrapped in greaseproof paper, parcelled up, and dispatched to New Guinea and beyond.[26]

Focusing on volunteer labour leads to a reassessment of women's roles, and concepts of work and citizenship in war-time. Analyses of women's roles in World War II have generally focused on the movement of women into paid employment. But whilst there were shifts in attitudes towards women taking paid employment due to the manpower shortages, it has been overstated. In 1943, at the peak of war-time paid employment, less than 32 per cent of available women (that is women between the ages of 15 and 65) or about 800 000 women were in paid work. Of that 32 per cent, only 2.4 per cent or 60 000 were in the auxiliary services.[27] What, therefore, were the majority of Australian women doing in World War II? They were busy taking unpaid work within their local communities as part of properly constituted organisations such as the Wallacia Comforts Club.

Another aspect of this theme is the changing relationship between the voluntary sector and government. An analysis of the Women's Voluntary National Register (WVNR) is an excellent example of this shifting relationship. The register was established by the Federal government in early 1939 after pressure from powerful women's groups wanting to be involved in what was at that time, war preparation. 'We, as you know, in the last war stood behind our men, but in this emergency we would like to stand with them', stated a defiant Mrs Mulcahy, president of the Returned Serviceman's League Central Women's Auxiliary, in February 1939 to the minister for defence, Brigadier Geoffrey Street.[28]

Run in a voluntary capacity for three years, the WVNR was eventually incorporated into the Manpower Directorate (that is taken over by government) in 1943. The majority of women who registered with the WVNR were between the ages of 17 and 35, and single. These women were volunteering to carry out unpaid work for the army, war-related patriotic funds, and businesses. Most had full-time employment and volunteered at nights and on weekends. The types of volunteer work ranged from the more traditional making comforts, unpicking uniforms, sewing, waitressing, cooking, nursing and orderly work; through typing, secretarial and general office work; to transport, navigators, engineering, and munitions work. Truda Davis, in her early 30s, undertook paid work at the Beaufort Bomber aircraft factory near Mascot in Sydney, working a 7 am to 4 pm shift five days a week. She then spent her evenings and weekends as a voluntary aid at Concord Repatriation Hospital. This was not an uncommon mix of paid and unpaid labour during the war.

The story of the WVNR is one of major transformation from voluntary to government action. The frontiers between paid and unpaid work, between government and voluntary spheres, all shifted and the relationship changed. The WVNR is also a good example of how women's volunteering provided the launching pad for women's entry into the paid workforce, a feature not usually emphasised in standard texts.

>━┥◆⟩━○━⟨◆┝━<

The memorial in Hyde Park is seldom empty, least of all on Anzac Day. Some come to pay a personal tribute, mourning friends and relatives lost in distant conflicts, others rise to a spirit of nationalism, many confess to a love of a parade. Cups of tea and refreshments are served by willing volunteer workers. Whatever the activity, and however diverse the individual motive, Anzac Day has become Australia's national festival, observed in virtually every community and marked, in recent years, by mass pilgrimages to battlefields overseas. A nation noted for its secularism has seized on Anzac Day with an almost religious fervour: in the words of one backpacker waiting for a cold dawn to break on Gallipoli, 'it's as close to sacred as Australians ever get'.[29]

Contrary to many predictions, the commemoration of Anzac did not end with the death of its veterans. Successive generations have reclaimed the memory of war, a rich 'composure' of the public and private, collective and individual histories. In the 1920s, Australians raised a forest of memorials vowing never to forget their sacrifice. Almost a century later, the memory remains as vivid, as complex, and as contested.

Notes

1 *The Book of the Anzac Memorial, New South Wales*, Sydney 1934, pp 47-50; 'Noble clay', *Sun*, 25 May 1932.

2 Bruce Scates and Rae Frances, *Women and the Great War*, Cambridge, 1997, ch 5; 'Anzac Memorial', *Sydney Morning Herald*, 15 July 1932.

3 Ken Inglis, *Sacred Places: war memorials in the Australian landscape*, Melbourne, 1998.

4 CEW Bean, *Official History of Australia in the War of 1914-18*, Sydney, 12 vols, 1937-42.

5 Marilyn Lake, 'Mission impossible: how men give birth to the Australian nation ~ gender, nationalism and other seminal acts', *Gender and History*, 4:3, 1992, pp 305-22; Bruce Scates, 'Imagining Anzac: children's memories of the killing fields of the Great War', in James Marten (ed), *Children and War: an historical anthology*, New York, 2002, pp 50-63; Peter Cochrane, *Simpson and the Donkey: the making of a legend*, Melbourne, 1992.

6 Joy Damousi and Marilyn Lake (eds), *Gender and War*, Melbourne, 1995; Jan Bassett, *Guns and Brooches*, Oxford, 1992.

7 CN Connolly, '"Manufacturing spontaneity": the Australian offers of troops for the Boer War', *Historical Studies*, 70, April 1978, pp 106-117; RL Wallace, *The Australians at the Boer War*, Canberra, 1976.

8 Craig Wilcox, *Australia's Boer War*, Melbourne, 2002.

9 Gavin Long et al, *Australia in the War of 1939-1945*, Canberra, 1952-1977 (5 series, 24 volumes).

10 Stephen Garton, *The Cost of War: Australians return*, Melbourne, 1996.

11 Richard White, 'War and Australian society', in M McKernan and M Browne (eds), *Australia: two centuries of peace and war*, Canberra, 1988.

12 Joan Beaumont, 'The state of Australian history of war', *Australian Historical Studies*, 121, April 2003, p 167.

13 Bill Gammage, *The Broken Years*, Canberra, 1974; Mark Johnston, *At the Front Line: experiences of Australian soldiers in World War Two*, Cambridge, 1996; Hank Nelson, *Chased by the Sun: courageous Australians in Bomber Command in World War II*, Sydney, 2001.

14 See any of the biographies published by Oxford University Press's Army History Series.

15 Bobbie Oliver, *Peacemongers: conscientious objectors to military service in Australia 1911-1945*, Fremantle, 1997; Christina Twomey, 'Impossible history: trauma and testimony among Australian civilians interned by the Japanese in World War Two', in Joy Damousi and Robert Reynolds (eds), *Histories of the Present: psychoanalysis, identity and the paradox of history*, Melbourne, 2004.

16 Damousi and Lake, *Gender and War*.

17 Alistair Thompson, *Anzac Memories: living with the legend*, Melbourne, 1994.

18 Anne Rutherford and James Wieland, *War: Australia's creative response*, Sydney, 1997.

19 Kate Darian-Smith, *On the Home Front: Melbourne in wartime 1939-1945*, Melbourne, 1990; John McQuilton, *Rural Australia and the Great War*, Melbourne, 2001.

20 Joy Damousi, *The Labour of Loss*, Cambridge, 1999, pp 48-49.

21 Cases of Privates M Docherty and FW Fox, Red Cross Wounded and Missing Files, Mortlock Library, SRG 76/1, Adelaide.

22 Bruce Scates, 'The unknown sock knitter: voluntary work, emotional labour, bereavement and the Great War', *Labour History*, 81, Nov 2001, pp 41-42.

23 Stéphane Audoin-Rouzeau and Annette Becker, *1914-1918: understanding the Great War*, London, 2002, p 204.

24 In Melanie Oppenheimer, *All Work No Pay: Australian civilian volunteers in war*, Walcha, 2002, p 43.

25 Melanie Oppenheimer, 'The best PM for the empire in war?: Lady Helen Munro Ferguson and the Australian Red Cross Society 1914-1920', *Australian Historical Studies*, 119, April 2002, pp 108-24.

26 Oppenheimer, *All Work No Pay*, p 91.

27 White, 'War and Australian society', pp 391-423.

28 Oppenheimer, *All Work No Pay*, p 104.

29 Bruce Scates, 'In Gallipoli's shadow: pilgrimage, memory, mourning and the Great War', *Australian Historical Studies*, 119, April 2002, p 8.

CHAPTER NINE

THE COMMON BOND?
AUSTRALIAN CITIZENSHIP

Alison Holland

Fifteen years ago, Australian citizenship was a neglected national theme; today it is at the centre of debate about Australia's future. Governments have looked to citizenship to fill a perceived civic deficit in the population and to construct cohesion in a diverse society. Less formally, concerns about citizenship were implicit in a cacophony of social and political discourses leading up to the Centenary of Federation in 2001. Central to these were the concerns about identity, belonging, nationhood and rights evident in all Western democracies faced with rapid social and economic change, and increasing diversity. Revived academic interest has sought to historicise citizenship and engage with international debates on citizenship's sustainability. For its part, the Federal government began the new century espousing the comforting line that Australian citizenship was 'the common bond at the heart of a unified and inclusive Australia'. This represented a profound contraction of the issues, problems, discourses and practices of citizenship which had escalated in the closing years of the twentieth century.

During those years, the Federal government established an Australian Citizenship Council. Its role was to advise on ways of celebrating the fiftieth anniversary of Australian citizenship in 1999 and prepare a report on policy and law. It was also to consider ways to promote an increased community awareness of citizenship, particularly as a unifying symbol. In its report, *Australian Citizenship for a New Century* (2000), the council recommended promoting citizenship not just as a legal category but in a much broader sense. It envisaged an Australian 'compact' proclaiming commitment to a set of core civic values, and saw the forthcoming Centenary of Federation as an opportunity to disseminate it, along with the Joint Parliamentary Statement on Racial Tolerance (1996) and the principles of Australian multiculturalism enunciated by the National Multicultural Advisory Council in 1999. Taken together, the council saw these statements as leading to a new civic definition of Australia.

The establishment of the council came at a critical juncture when the meaning and practice of citizenship were being contested in a variety of forums. It flowed from over a decade of governmental concern and a bipartisan commitment to promote active citizenship. Heated debates over history, republicanism, Indigenous rights and identity, ethnicity, multiculturalism and refugees, conducted against the background of a powerful resurgence of racism, gave voice to widespread anxiety over the changing complexion of Australian society. Central to this change was the increasing visibility of Indigenous and ethnic minorities and their demand for recognition and rights. In the conservative backlash which ensued, there was a strong yearning for an assimilationist past, where differences, particularly cultural ones, could be forgotten or lost, and where citizenship was uncomplicated by the rights of 'others'.

In part, the Citizenship Council saw its task as responding to public uncertainty about what Australians held in common. They noted that multiculturalism had destabilised society to the extent that old national symbols seemed less relevant and, despite the 'success' of the policy, there was a lingering community suspicion that diversity could lead to socially harmful division. There was talk of 'ethnic neighbourhoods' challenging the traditional dominance of society's Anglo-Celtic foundations. These concerns are symptomatic of what Kymlicka and Norman identify as 'citizenship worries' manifest in many Western liberal democracies faced with the challenge of ethnocultural diversity and the potentially differentiated citizenship status which it implies.[1] The council believed that the promotion of a national civic compact could overcome this 'worry' by focusing on core values all could share, irrespective of diversity. These included commitment to the land, to the rule of law and equality under the law, to the basics of representative democracy, to principles of tolerance and fairness, to acceptance of cultural diversity, to the well-being of all Australians, and to recognising the unique status of Aborigines and Torres Strait Islanders. Furthermore, it believed that a civic definition could replace the obsession with national identity which it saw as constantly changing, potentially exclusive and divisive. In this sense, the polity rather than the nation would become the focus of belonging.

Citing lack of community demand, the government shelved the council's recommendations. It remained silent on the dissemination of the statement on racial tolerance and rejected the close link between the promotion of civic values and multiculturalism, arguing that the two could remain separate. Instead it saw the forthcoming Centenary of Federation celebrations as a means of encouraging the 950 000 permanent residents to take up citizenship and declared an annual day of celebration. It sub-titled its report *A Common Bond* to drive home the central idea of a citizenship 'designed to reinforce the benefits of unity'.

Subjects of the empire

Yet for most of the twentieth century, citizenship signalled unity only inasmuch as it symbolised the primacy of Anglo-Saxonness. Surprisingly, from an international perspective, the federation of the previously six separate colonies (now termed states) into the Australian Commonwealth in 1901 was a painless birth when it came to citizenship. Although, as Chesterman and Galligan point out, the creation of an Australian citizenship was also one of Federation's achievements, it was implied rather than explicitly stated.[2] The Australian Constitution was more concerned with the power of governments –

the respective responsibilities of the states and commonwealth – than with the rights and obligations of citizens. Nowhere is there a definition of citizenship in the Constitution. Nor is there any explicit protection of human rights, as in Canada and New Zealand. Unlike the American War of Independence, Federation marked no abrupt break with the past. It was a conservative restatement of the status quo: people born in Australia together with those who were naturalised became British subjects.

Australia's self-identification as 'British' well into the twentieth century has had significant ramifications for citizenship.[3] Although the Federal government was concerned to shape a distinctive Australian citizenry from 1901, the primary focus was on maintaining the 'crimson thread of kinship' to the empire. All people born in Australia (including Aborigines) became British subjects from the moment the Crown assumed sovereignty in 1788. British subjecthood was thought to provide the necessary apparatus for a cohesive and loyal citizenry that would shore up Australia's defences against potential enemies within and without. This notion of protecting the internal and external borders of the nation was particularly pertinent at the turn of the twentieth century when, as elsewhere, there was a powerful confluence of discourses concerning national fitness, race, reproduction and civilisation. In this context, the principal source of unity for most of the twentieth century was racial exclusivity, encoded in the *Immigration Restriction Act* (1901), which targeted non-Europeans. The administrative silence on citizenship, then, was premised on racial exclusion.

If the language of citzenship was absent from the Constitution, it was not insignificant in broader social and political disputes of the period. The last decades of the nineteenth century saw a variety of experiments in social welfare which defined the rights and entitlements of members of the community and the responsibilities of the state. Pensions and other schemes for the relief of poverty shifted from the hands of private charity to those of governments and, in the process, the grounds for entitlement were increasingly understood in terms of the contribution of workers, mothers, soldiers and children to the greater good of the present and future society. Australasia (including New Zealand) briefly developed an international reputation as a 'social laboratory' for experiments in welfare and citizenship, and the prevalence of a discourse of self-conscious pride in this respect perhaps sparked further demands.

White feminists, in particular, self-consciously articulated their demands within a rhetoric of citizenship. From the late nineteenth century, they sought equal citizenship (principally the vote) in order to advance the particular cause of women and provide a woman-centred approach to public life. But they did so because women's lives were so heavily circumscribed by masculine dominance, and they suffered high levels of physical abuse, drunkenness and desertion. In a recent history of Australian feminism in which the politics of these 'first-wave' feminists are recovered, Marilyn Lake argues that they saw in equal citizenship a means of political and economic equality, equality in moral standards, bodily inviolability, and the protection of married women's nationality.[4] For the feminists the independence of the married woman was pivotal, not only to women's freedom but also in advancing women's service to the state – their maternal citizenship.[5]

While Lake argues for the feminists' success, the key 'success' of the welfare state is still represented as the basic or 'family' wage, won by the white male worker and enshrined in the Harvester Judgment of 1907 – when Justice Higgins in the newly created Arbitration Court set the basic wage to be paid to workers in a harvester factory. Giving legal definition to the minimum male workers' wage as one that was sufficient to support wife and three children, this judgment provided a legacy of gender differentiation which continues to devalue the work of women in the domestic economy.[6]

While women at the turn of the century achieved political recognition of their rights to citizenship, albeit in a form that stressed their continued dependence and need for protection, for another key group the impact of Federation was far more destructive.

Patricia Grimshaw identifies Federation as a 'turning point' for Aborigines in that it extinguished a promised path to citizenship.[7] In the nineteenth century, British humanitarians had promised, albeit under the guise of the 'civilising mission', a pathway to civil rights which included entitlement to reserves and compensation. This had already begun to fade with the acquisition of colonial self-government in the second half of the nineteenth century. At Federation, Aborigines were effectively written out of the nation altogether. Just as women gained the federal vote in 1902 under the *Commonwealth Franchise Act*, Aborigines were simultaneously denied it. The Constitution dictated that they were not to be counted in the national census. Further, they were to be locked in a state of 'domestic' dependence via state government control. This effectively gave the states *carte blanche*, shutting out the possibility of external scrutiny, for, constitutionally, only the Commonwealth government is held accountable at the international level.

Not surprisingly, it was the quest for equal citizenship that dominated the Aboriginal struggle in the twentieth century. This was because it had to, so profound was the civil, political and economic discrimination against them after Federation. As Heather Goodall has effectively demonstrated, citizen rights became the *a priori* defence of Indigenous people's land and collective rights.[8] The status of Aborigines for most of the twentieth century demonstrates the hollowness of Australian citizenship. Although classified as British subjects and, after 1948, Australian citizens (see below), Aborigines were effectively citizens without rights. Subject to constant surveillance and policing, Aboriginal lives were held captive by the state. Every aspect of their lives, their residence, work and pay, movement, mode of living, family relations, marriage partners, even death, was dictated by state-initiated 'protection' and later 'welfare' laws. The penalties for protest were severe. Nor did they have access to the benefits of the welfare state. It was not until the late 1950s that Aborigines could benefit from the full range of social rights.

Aliens within and without

Clearly, Federation in 1901 was an ambiguous 'compact' when it came to citizenship. But, according to a recent history of citizenship by David Dutton, World War I was a key galvanizing moment in citizenship policy.[9] It was during that war that the Australian government demonstrated a willingness to forgo certain citizen rights, particularly in terms of free speech and thought, by ushering in special defence legislation against popular opposition. Dutton cites the emergence of new criteria for eligibility in immigration and naturalisation at this time as demonstrating a concern with the entry of potentially threatening political values and beliefs. Further, he identifies the war as a stark retreat from more cosmopolitan nineteenth-century ideas and policies about the relatively small European populations in Australia. It was during the war, he argues, that foreigners were reconceptualised in close relation to subversion and disloyalty. Non-British Europeans were now thought of as potentially dangerous, as illustrated by the internment of 'enemy aliens' and the dispersal and assimilation of alien communities throughout Australia during and after the war.

World War I also played a major role in promoting ideals of masculine and feminine citizenship that continue to resonate. In Chapter Eight, Oppenheimer and Scates show the resilience of the masculinist Anzac tradition which enshrined the (non-Aboriginal) soldier as the archetypal Australian citizen. The power and persistence of this model has had ramifications for female citizenship. Feminist historians have pointed out the importance of the concept of the citizen mother for female identity in Australia. Women's role as (white) mothers of the nation was particularly evident post-Federation, as, in the light of decreased fertility rates, there was concern about the numerical strength and fitness of the population. The exigencies of national defence merely heightened this. But, as Crawford and Maddern argue, Australian concepts of child-bearing in relation to citizenship have implied a distinction between the citizen-mother and the citizen-soldier, so that although both roles are constituted as a national service, child-bearing and rearing are often accorded a lower citizenship value.[10] The contemporary discourse on low fertility rates reveals the long shadow cast by World War I. Women are being exhorted to have more babies despite the lack of material incentive for doing so.[11] The point is, Margaret Thornton suggests, that good mothering in the private sphere still represents the realisation of women's effective citizenship.[12]

It is not generally recognised that the war was also a factor influencing new directions in Aboriginal policy. Following the war there was a heightened consideration of the Aborigines' place in the nation's future. This focus was generated by concern over the rise of a mixed-race population. But it was also conditioned by the persistence of an Aboriginal majority in the north which continued to make its presence felt in intermittent cases of inter-racial conflict. At the same time, dispossessed Aboriginal populations in the south were clamouring for citizen rights, which was as much a recognition of difference as a demand for equality. The need to solve these seemingly intractable 'problems' was felt with some urgency after the war because of a heightened fear that racial conflict was now the biggest threat to a fragile world peace. In Australia, administrators determined on a policy change from protectionism to assimilation, from cultural stasis to cultural absorption or extinction, and the ultimate denial of Aboriginality altogether.

The war, therefore, demonstrated how far the national government was prepared to go to override the civil and political rights of citizens in the interests of national security and defence – internal and external. It showed how ideas of race and nationality underpinned and legitimised violations of such rights. It demonstrated at once the significance (from a liberal governance perspective) and potential insignificance (from a citizen's perspective) of citizenship to the nation state. It demonstrated that the state was not beyond using violence in the interests of social cohesion, and that difference (racial, cultural, political) constituted the biggest threat to it.

Furthermore, the war set a precedent: once established, actions and processes could be, and were, replicated in times of national emergency or apparent threat. Davidson shows the implications of this in the area of industrial and political organisation from the 1930s to the 1950s, from the detention of political prisoners to the attempted banning of the Communist Party in the 1950s.[13] And, as Bashford and Strange have argued, the practice of alien internment provided the setting for the mass incarceration without trial of people who had committed no crime.[14] They argue that such confinement finds resonance in the contemporary mandatory detention of asylum seekers. Such practices illustrate the emptiness of British subjecthood/Australian citizenship which ultimately provided no protection or rights for citizens.

Multiculturalism with mono-nationality

It was not until after World War II that the legal category of 'Australian citizen' came into being, again without fanfare. Indeed, on 26 January 1949 the majority of the Australian population was officially designated Australian citizens (and British subjects simultaneously until 1984) without knowledge of the fact. The civil and political rights associated with being a 'natural born British subject' were simply rolled over when citizen status was officially bestowed with the passing of the *Nationality and Citizenship Act* in 1948. And the distinctive feature of Australian citizenship, born out of the Federation years – the separation of formal citizenship status from rights and benefits and the emphasis on common law protection and government provision – remained in place. In other words, despite specific legislation citizenship remained, and remains, ill-defined.

Coinciding as it did with the drive to lift Australia's population after 1945, the *Nationality and Citizenship Act* was primarily concerned with the naturalisation of non-British migrants, mostly refugees and others from war-torn Europe (90 per cent of the population were of Anglo-Celtic descent in 1947 when the first government-assisted 'alien' immigrant arrived in Australia). The Act differentiated between British subjects (including Irish citizens and protected persons) and all others, who were defined as 'aliens'. It gave preferential treatment to the former and demanded assimilation of the latter.

As a doctrine of national unity, assimilation rested on assumptions of race and nationality which promoted sameness and homogeneity. Migrants – 'New Australians' – were not only actively discriminated against but were expected to leave their old cultures and allegiances behind and absorb 'the Australian way of life'. They were required to demonstrate renunciation of prior allegiance (familial, social, economic and political) with 'others' of foreign birth to qualify for naturalisation. This conflation of nationality and allegiance was evident in citizenship policy as early as 1917, when it was first introduced by the Commonwealth Government, and as late as 1984 when it was finally abolished. These ideas continued to find resonance, however, in the treatment of dual nationality.

Until April 2002, Australian citizens were prevented from holding dual nationality, automatically forfeiting their citizen status upon naturalisation in another country. Even then the fine print meant that for some nothing had changed. This is remarkably backward when compared with many other Western democracies with which Australia likes to compare itself. As Dutton suggests, it goes to the heart of conceptions of citizenship in Australia because it is ultimately about allegiance. Dual citizenship was anathema to successive Australian governments for whom divided loyalties were unthinkable and social cohesion demanded a citizenry free of internal divisions and bound by a common identity.[15] The indissolubility of Australian citizenship status demonstrates how concepts of allegiance and nationality, pertinent to an assimilationist framework, persisted into the new millennium.

Conversely, it demonstrates the limits of multiculturalism. Had multiculturalism penetrated the boundaries of citizenship policy more fully in the last quarter of the twentieth century, dual citizenship for Australian citizens might well have been legalised much sooner. Cultural pluralism, at the very least, recognises the possibility of multiple identities and allegiances. Certainly, when multiculturalism became government policy in 1973, the hope was that the make-up of post-war Australian society would be more adequately represented and that diversity would be recognised and respected. Legislation matched this new conception of the national citizenry by removing the various distinctions and anomalies – principally residency and English language requirements – between British subjects and all others, defined as permanent residents from 1975. These structural changes were gradually matched by infrastructural changes to meet migrant need, but not by any substantive changes to citizenship as theory or practice.

Indeed, there is broad agreement that multiculturalism has not significantly altered the fundamental fabric of Australian society. As Wills suggests, the emphasis has been on ways of controlling diversity in order to render it subservient to the already constituted nationalist imagination.[16] By and large this is premised on the superiority of the Anglo-Celtic majority, despite the radically altered complexion of the population in the last 50 years – since the *Nationality and Citizenship Act* in 1948 Australia has accepted over three million migrants from 180 different countries. Davidson shows how the notion of belonging to the 'one big family' recurs in phases of resurgent nationalism, like the 1980s and 1990s, working to limit receptivity to broader ideas about citizenship from overseas.[17] He and others are critical of celebratory accounts of multiculturalism in the face of entrenched Anglo-Celtic institutional foundations and what Davidson describes as the continued silencing of the migrant voice.[18] They point to the extremely limited nature of the resurgent republicanism of the 1990s, when emphasis was on the appointment of an Australian head of state above all else.

Furthermore, as the recurrent debates on immigration demonstrate, multiculturalism has never sat comfortably in the Australian moral and political landscape. Critics abound. From the conservative standpoint, multiculturalism ultimately disrupts the fixation with unity. There is fear that it leads to social division, entrenches cultural difference and champions ethnic separatism. Those on the Left question accounts of multicultural success because they hide social inequalities and racism. Ghassan Hage's demand for a deeper commitment to multiculturalism and to the decentralising effects of migration and globalisation, while not alone, is marginal.[19] Advocates from both sides of the political spectrum seek to downplay or abolish multiculturalism. For the conservative majority, now widely termed 'mainstream', this amounts to a preference for national homogeneity and monoculturalism. On the other hand, the Australian Citizenship Council's emphasis on a civic definition of Australia points to an unease, amongst some academics, with ethnically based policies.

There is dissatisfaction about the lack of substance to citizenship in general. The real problem, from a multicultural perspective, is not the acquisition of citizenship but the gulf between the legal and social definitions of citizenship. Most critics concede that new immigrants can obtain Australian citizenship very easily. Qualifications are amongst the most liberal in the world. While Hage argues that citizenship, at least for Arab Australians, is not about rights so much as responsibility, some see rights, or the lack thereof, as central to the problem.

Jayasuriya sees the main problem as the lack of any substantive recognition of minority or group rights that would allow for a form of citizenship which recognises specificity or difference.[20] Without legal or constitutional safeguards directly applicable to citizenship, minority or group rights are left to the common law and the political and social institutions of governments. A strong tradition of resistance to differential treatment for various groups of citizens has permitted very few group-based legislative enactments. Jayasuriya also points to the distinctive Australian tradition of strong 'industrial' citizenship, whereby social rights are equated with economic rights. In this context the rights of citizenship, particularly of ethnic minorities, are minimised by a dominant tradition of labourism and the welfare state. Like other commentators, Jayasuriya's concern is with the limitations of liberal democratic citizenship as offering at best an assimilationist and at worst a racist model of identity.

There has been revived academic interest of late in assimilation and particularly in its grip on the minds of many Australians.[21] Dutton emphasises the fixity of the core culture throughout the twentieth century.[22] He argues that race and allegiance continued to be the basic condition of citizenship, despite changes to understandings of human difference and a changed discourse in which race rarely featured. This is remarkable when one thinks of the scale of the population change since the 1950s. It demonstrates a central feature of citizenship in Australia: in official terms, from Federation on, citizenship has been an extremely pragmatic exercise, largely designed to increase the body count and to shore up Australia's defences. The change from a pledge of allegiance to a pledge of commitment in 1993 (omitting mention of the British monarch for the first time) is merely a contemporary concession to an old and enduring ideal of loyalty. The central question remains the same: do you count yourself in or out?

Indigenous citizenship and rights

It is in the area of Indigenous rights – land and culture – that we see the continued relevance of race and allegiance most clearly. Any appraisal of the Aboriginal quest for citizenship must also emphasise their struggle for Indigenous rights. Tim Rowse argues that both the rhetoric of citizenship based on industry, and the promise of equality, have worked to obscure the particularity of Indigenous rights.[23] As in other settler societies of the British Commonwealth, the belated recognition of these has transformed the politics of ethnicity in Australia over the past decade. The recognition of native title in the Mabo and Wik decisions of 1992 and 1996 respectively has been the most fundamental challenge to Australia's legal system, because it displaces the basis of settler sovereignty over Aborigines. This was based on the European settlement of vacant or under-utilised land. The rights of first discovery infiltrated the very fabric of the white settler state. It was the basis of its history, legitimacy and citizenship. From the 1970s, however, revisionist histories have uncovered Aboriginal and non-Aboriginal acknowledgment of Aboriginal custodianship of land from 1788.[24] These have been augmented more recently with environmental histories which have recovered the intricate land and resource management of Aboriginal populations.[25] This re-writing of the past has been profoundly unsettling for the settler state, as the history wars attest.

The formal acknowledgment of land rights also challenges thinking about Aborigines as citizens for it recognises rights peculiar to them. Any concept of differentiated citizenship status which recognises Indigenous collective rights, such as sovereignty, has been strongly resisted. Indeed, Paul Havemann sees Australia as a special case in this regard, pointing to precedents in New Zealand and Canada in which indigenous rights are at least given formal recognition in national law.[26] In Australia, how Indigenous rights relate to citizenship arouses ongoing debate.[27]

In the twentieth century, Indigenous activists had a twin conception of their struggle: there was the quest for equal citizenship (and the civil, political and social rights which accrue), and the quest for land and the collective, cultural rights which go with this. Fundamentally, their struggles aimed at the recognition of their human rights, as the outspoken Aboriginal rights' activist, Mary Bennett, so astutely wrote in 1930.[28] Despite their interconnectedness – one struggle informing the other – there is debate over the extent to which Indigenous peoples' demand for equality in citizenship displaced their demand for collective rights based in land.[29]

The justification for the violation of Indigenous rights was that 'as a backward people' Aborigines were subject to special laws as protective measures. Perversely, like interned enemy aliens, their citizenship status was never in doubt. The close connection between civilisation and citizenship prescribed that Aborigines be made fit for the latter. As a number of historians have pointed out, this view was so pervasive that, by and large, Aboriginal activists believed it too. Indeed, their *capacity* for citizenship was constantly invoked. But it was so because, despite many of them meeting the requirements of citizenship, they were consistently denied its rewards. The best example here is the use of Aboriginal men as servicemen during war and their subsequent denial of any privileges as returned soldiers. Like interned enemy aliens, Aborigines were treated as they were because of the dictates of racial exclusion. Nowhere was this clearer than in the requirement that, should they wish to be free of state control, they could apply for exemption from 'the Act'. However, exemption required total rejection of their Aboriginality, particularly their allegiance to kith, kin and culture.

Few accepted this pathway to liberation. Yet, while they abhorred and protested against the style of protection they were offered, they didn't reject protection out of hand. The most obvious sense in which Aborigines understood the specificity of their claims and the need for their accommodation by the settler state, against a broader demand for equality, was in the manner of their protest. There is a tradition in the Aboriginal quest for rights in which they appeal to the highest authorities of state, including the British monarch. Underwriting this tradition is an understanding that they are owed just treatment, compensation, citizenship and land because of their status as a colonised minority. Indeed, there is a sense in which they believe that recognition of this fact constitutes a non-Aboriginal person's *citizen* responsibility. Related to this is the way in which they requested citizenship. Aboriginal activism did not coalesce in demands for the vote, like that of white women, despite the long-held desire for Aboriginal representation in parliament. Instead, they wanted the 'grant' of citizenship. Again, this was viewed as compensation for loss.

This is partly why the 1967 referendum was mythologised as the marker of Aboriginal citizenship. In 1967 non-Aboriginal Australians overwhelmingly voted to remove two discriminatory clauses from the Constitution. Aborigines were now to be counted in the census, and the Commonwealth was given the power to make laws on their behalf. For so long had Aborigines seen this as central to their liberation from state power that it was automatically celebrated as delivery of their long-awaited rights. But, as recent revision has shown, the 1967 referendum delivered no such thing.[30] It did not repeal state legislation. It did not even *require* Commonwealth control, it merely gave it conjoint power with the states to legislate on their behalf – something it was reluctant to do.

Aborigines were never formally granted citizenship primarily because respective governments continued to argue that they already had it. 1967 became a convenient smokescreen for a national government smarting under the weight of national and international pressure on 'race'. Indeed, it was this pressure, according to Chesterman, which accounted for the delivery of key civil rights such as the vote, social security and wages, and the gradual dismantling of the specific legislation targeting them from the mid-1960s.[31] Aborigines obtained 'real' citizenship by sleight of hand and, as for non-Aborigines, it counted for little. After over eighty years of demands for a definition of Aboriginal citizenship, the terms of Aboriginal inclusion and status in the nation are left vague.

⊳━◀▸━○━◂▸━◀

As this history suggests, there have been notable and passionate battles for citizenship, despite the oft-repeated conclusion that there is an emptiness at its heart. The practice of silencing the 'ethnic other', for example, replicates a historic tradition of silencing demands for a citizenship which recognised both equality and difference for women and for Aborigines. The salience of assimilationist thinking was evident here too. Women had to accept citizenship within an entrenched patriarchal system while Aborigines accepted theirs within a patriarchal *and* colonial state. Despite their formal citizenship and, in the case of Aborigines, the recognition of native title, their joint struggles were unfinished by the close of the twentieth century.

For Aborigines, the non-Aboriginal population left the twentieth century without complete comprehension of the nature, meaning and history of their struggle. For women, the close of the twentieth century saw a renewed appreciation of the power and persistence of the late nineteenth-century feminist struggle and the conditions which gave it birth. For, although Australian women were among the first (white) women in the world to gain the vote, they have yet to attain full equality. Furthermore, there is mounting criticism of a regression of women's rights in the closing stages of the twentieth century, despite the gains of post-1960s feminism. Veteran feminist Anne Summers argues that in all aspects of women's lives the ideal of non-discrimination has not been met.[32] Women's access to full-time paid work, childcare, maternity payments and opportunities for leadership in the public and private sectors, along with the prevalence of sexual and domestic violence, illustrates the resonance of the late nineteenth-century feminist campaigns in the present.

On the other hand, how to incorporate ethnic diversity remains a key and pressing issue. By the 1990s, many of the old symbols of (assimilationist) unity – belief in Anglo-Saxonness, White Australia, 'the bush' - had faded. But what had replaced them? Despite the shift in official rhetoric from assimilation to multiculturalism in the last quarter of the twentieth century, there have been no consistent or coherent symbols to take their place. The Federal government's refusal to invest value and meaning into citizenship in terms of the lived experience of its citizenry demonstrates a pragmatism characteristic of the conservative tradition.

The Australian Citizenship Council argued that the way to achieve social cohesion was via the engagement and negotiation of difference, and as in the statement on racial tolerance, the recognition of rights. This was unlikely to be implemented by a governing Liberal-National coalition dominated by an Anglo-Celtic majority harbouring a deep tradition of racism and xenophobia.[33] In fact, by disconnecting civic values from multicultural ones, the contemporary Federal government looked back to a pre-multicultural society where difference, with its potential for disunity, was treated with suspicion and paranoia. In this context, the 'common bond' is more likely to reflect (rhetorically) its original meaning – the bond of British nationality. As Alastair Davidson emphasises, among conservative leaders there is a belief in the superiority of British traditions and all that they stand for. Of particular significance for citizenship is a suspicion of rights discourse and a belief in the sufficiency of the British common law tradition in protecting the rights of citizens.

The Citizenship Council's 'compact' represented an opportunity to infuse some definition into the terms of Australian citizenship and, more importantly, to show leadership on this issue. But, unsurprisingly given its complex history, a huge gap became apparent between the ideas and possibilities envisaged for citizenship promoted from within the academy, of which the Citizenship Council's 'compact' is an offshoot, and the 'vision' promoted by the national government. The current government's insistence on the compulsory singing of national anthems and raising of flags in public schools to instil civic pride, while at the same time silencing dissent and closing off possibilities for public debate on this issue, represents a recrudescent nationalism, evident from the 1980s, which ultimately promotes a provincial, parochial standard of the nation. One is left to conclude that the lack of definition of citizenship has served most Australian governments well. It remains to be seen whether it will continue to do so into the future.

Notes

I would like to thank Lisa Featherstone for providing valuable research assistance, and Mary Spongberg for her support in the preparation of this chapter.

1   Will Kymlicka and Wayne Norman (eds), *Citizenship in Diverse Societies*, Oxford, 2000, p 31.

2   John Chesterman and Brian Galligan, *Defining Australian Citizenship*, Melbourne, 1999, p 1.

3   David Dutton, *One of Us? a century of Australian citizenship*, Sydney, 2002, p 10.

4   Marilyn Lake, *Getting Equal: the history of Australian feminism*, Sydney, 1999.

5   Marilyn Lake, 'A revolution in the family: the challenge and contradictions of maternal citizenship in Australia', in Seth Koven and Sonya Michel (eds), *Mothers of a New World: maternalist politics and the origins of welfare states*, London, 1993, pp 378-95.

6   Tim Rowse, *White Flour, White Power: from rations to citizenship in Central Australia*, Melbourne, 1998, p 117.

7   Pat Grimshaw, 'Federation as a turning point in Australian history', *Australian Historical Studies*, no 118, 2002.

8   Goodall, *Invasion to Embassy: land in Aboriginal politics in New South Wales 1770-1972*, Sydney, 1996.

9   Dutton, *One of Us?*, p 148.

10 Patricia Crawford and Philippa Maddern (eds), *Women as Australian Citizens: underlying histories*, Melbourne, 2001, p 211.

11 Anne Summers, *The End of Equality: work, babies and women's choices in 21st century Australia*, Sydney, 2003.

12 Margaret Thornton, 'Legal citizenship' in Wayne Hudson and John Kane (eds), *Rethinking Australian Citizenship*, Melbourne, 2000, p 118.

13 Alastair Davidson, *From Subject to Citizen: Australian citizenship in the 20th century*, Melbourne, 1997, pp 84-112.

14 Alison Bashford and Carolyn Strange, 'Asylum-seekers and national histories of detention', *Australian Journal of Politics and History*, 48:4, 2002, p 518.

15 Dutton, *One of Us?*, p 157.

16 Sara Wills, 'Un-stitching the lips of a migrant nation', *Australian Historical Studies*, 33:118, 2002, p 72.

17 Davidson, *From Subject to Citizen*, pp 105-108.

18 Alastair Davidson, 'Multiculturalism and citizenship: silencing the migrant voice', *Journal of Intercultural Studies*, 18:2, 1997, pp 77-92; Stephen Castles, 'Multicultural citizenship: a response to the dilemma of globalization and national identity?', *Journal of Intercultural Studies*, 18:1, 1997, pp 5-22.

19 Ghassan Hage, *White Nation: fantasies of white supremacy in a multicultural society*, Sydney, 1998.

20 Laksiri Jayasuriya, 'Citizens', in Richard Nile (ed), *Australian Civilisation*, Melbourne, 1994, pp 93-109.

21 Anna Haebich, 'Imagining assimilation', *Australian Historical Studies*, no 118, 2002, pp 61-70; Tim Rowse (ed), *Contesting Assimilation: histories of colonial and Indigenous initiatives*, 2005.

22 Dutton, *One of Us?*, p 154.

23 Rowse, *White Flour*, pp 210-213.

24 Henry Reynolds, *The Law of the Land*, Melbourne, 2003; Lyndall Ryan, *The Aboriginal Tasmanians*, Sydney, 1996.

25 David Horton, *Pure State of Nature: sacred cows, destructive myths and the environment*, Sydney, 2000; Jim Kohen, *Aboriginal Environmental Impacts*, Sydney, 1995.

26 Paul Havemann, 'Comparing Indigenous peoples' rights in Australia, Canada

and New Zealand: some signposts', in Paul Havemann (ed), *Indigenous Peoples' Rights in Australia, Canada and New Zealand*, Auckland, 1999.

27 Kim Rubenstein (ed), *Individual Community Nation: 50 years of Australian citizenship*, Melbourne, 2000, pp 68-71.

28 Mary Bennett, *The Australian Aboriginal as a Human Being*, London, 1930.

29 Bain Attwood, *Rights for Aborigines*, Sydney, 2003; Russell McGregor, 'Protest and progress: Aboriginal activism in the 1930s', *Australian Historical Studies*, no 101, October, 1993, pp 555-68.

30 Bain Attwood and Andrew Markus, 'Representation matters: the 1967 referendum and citizenship', in Nicolas Peterson and Will Sanders (eds), *Citizenship and Indigenous Australians: changing conceptions and possibilities*, Melbourne, 1998, pp 118-40.

31 John Chesterman, 'Defending Australia's reputation: how Indigenous Australians won civil rights', *Australian Historical Studies*, 32:116 and 32:117, 2001, pp 20-39 and 201-21 (two articles).

32 Summers, *The End of Equality*, pp 1-17.

33 Davidson, *From Subject to Citizen*, p 97.

CHAPTER TEN

CITIES, SUBURBS AND COMMUNITIES

Seamus O'Hanlon

Australia's self-image, and that which it projects to the world, is of a rural people more at home sleeping under the stars or wrestling crocodiles than engaging in daily battle with the noise, traffic and congestion of the city. Yet the reality is that Australia is one of the most urbanised societies in the world. About 85 per cent of the population live and work in cities or towns of 1000 or more residents. More than 40 per cent live within about 200 kilometres of the two largest cities, Sydney and Melbourne. This has long been the case. The various state and territory capitals plus a few other smaller cities have dominated Australian national life for more than a century, possibly since the 1820s. Yet until relatively recently the cities were largely absent from the Australian story, including Australian historiography, which privileged an idealised rural past over the urban reality. This absence of urban history from Australian discourses was not unusual, as it was only in the 1960s and 1970s that the study of urban history and the day-to-day lives of urban communities came under sustained academic scrutiny in most Western nations. But, for a variety of reasons, the absence was more extreme in Australia than most other places.

Understanding the cities is, I would argue, central to any understanding of Australia's past and present. But while Australians are urbanites, the lived experience of most Australia city-dwellers has been overwhelmingly suburban, so much so that the country's foremost urban historian Graeme Davison has challenged American Kenneth Jackson's assertion that the United States was the world's first suburban nation, arguing that Australia more rightly deserves that possibly dubious honour.[1] It is therefore to the suburbs, and the profound Australian belief in the 'Great Australian Dream' of a stand-alone owner-occupied home, that the historian should turn to understand and explain Australia's urban past.

But before we begin that task, a word of explanation about terminology. International observers need to be aware that the terms 'city' and 'suburb' are in many ways interchangeable in the Australian context. Unlike in Europe and North America, there is no legal differentiation between the two entities, and Australia's metropolitan areas are composed of suburbs grouped into municipalities (usually called 'cities'), each able to raise revenue through household rates to pay for local services such as garbage collection, street cleaning and general urban maintenance. Essential services such as education and health, on the other hand, are provided at state level, meaning that while there are wealthier and poorer districts within Australian metropolitan areas, there is not the vast gulf between the classes seen in cities elsewhere in the world. To avoid confusion on this issue, throughout this chapter I have used the terms 'city' to refer to metropolitan areas, 'suburb' to refer to individual suburbs ('neighborhood' in the North American context), and 'inner urban' or 'inner city', to refer to older inner-urban areas, especially, but not exclusively in Sydney and Melbourne.

The forgotten city

To a present-day observer, the economic and social pre-eminence of cities in Australian history may seem unproblematic, but until the 1960s this idea was a profound, indeed challenging, concept. Until then Australian history, if it was studied at all, examined political institutions, the rise of the labour movement, and the slow emergence of an Australian as distinct from British attitude and outlook.

Australian history privileged an idealised, masculinist, 'bush' story that depicted the cities as parasitical entities living off the bounty provided by rural men and the wool and mining industries. The cities were seen as feminine, the concerns of city-dwellers, 'soft', shallow and irredeemably domestic in scope, and hardly the stuff of history. Even after World War II, when Australian history began to gain some academic respectability, the cities were ignored. In Russel Ward's highly influential 1958 book, *The Australian Legend*, the cities appear only fleetingly, and their role in the creation of an Australian national identity is mainly to drain wealth and the makings of a masculine, nationalist culture from the less-populous rural regions.

It was a non-Australian who first recognised the importance of cities in Australian history. In his 1963 study, *Victorian Cities*, British historian Asa Briggs included Melbourne as a 'Victorian community overseas' and saw, in its rapid nineteenth-century growth and development, strong echoes of the urbanisation of Britain in the Industrial Revolution. Briggs, who had spent time in Australia in 1961, recognised that like Manchester and Middlesbrough, colonial Melbourne was a product of the expansion of British trade and industry, and the story of its phenomenal growth from nothing to a city of half a million in fifty years was of significance, not only in Australian, but world terms. In the 1960s Australian historians, led by economic historian Noel Butlin, also began to challenge received ideas about the historical importance of the rural economy in the country's development. Butlin's work, and that of fellow economic historians, most notably John McCarty, demonstrated that city-building and associated enterprises were important components of Australia's economic growth in the nineteenth century, potentially rivalling rural industries in domestic economic importance. In the 1970s, McCarty further developed the idea of the economic importance of Australian cities by demonstrating that they were commercial entrepots for the hinterlands of the various colonies. The cities, with their commercial links to the British Empire, were the locus of colonisation, settlement and development, according to McCarty, and were therefore the drivers of economic development and expansion, rather than the parasitic entities formerly assumed.

From the 1960s, the cities moved to the centre of Australian historiography. Economic historians followed Butlin and McCarty's lead and wrote on the economy of the cities, while Graeme Davison combined economic and social history to report on the experience of Melbourne's spectacular boom and equally spectacular bust in the 1880s and 1890s.[2] He and other younger historians around the country followed up with a series of studies on the history of the cities, mostly concentrating on the period of rapid urban growth in the late nineteenth century. The emphasis was now firmly on social history and the lived experience of ordinary people – 'history from below', or perhaps from the back streets. Few historians were prepared to venture into the twentieth century, perhaps because it was too familiar to be of interest historically, but also perhaps because the story of the twentieth century Australian city was the story of the expansion of suburbia, again hardly the stuff of history. The most important exception to this absence was Peter Spearritt, whose *Sydney since the Twenties* (Sydney, 1978) tells the story of the expansion of the city outwards, but also upwards as Sydney cemented its place as Australia's pre-eminent commercial city by the 1970s.

A striking feature of urban history in Australia, especially, but not exclusively in Melbourne, has been accessible local and community history written by academics and professional historians. With the notable exception of Geoffrey Blainey's work on Camberwell and Weston Bate's on Brighton – both middle-class Melbourne suburbs – academically written local histories traditionally reflected the social history ethos and were about the 'other' – close-knit, high-density, working-class inner-city communities – rather than suburbia, the habitat of the majority of Australians. Middle-class, suburban community histories were usually, although not exclusively, the province of professional historians commissioned to write incisive, but invariably celebratory, histories marking municipal anniversaries and milestones. A more recent generation of urban historians has challenged this idea of telling an over-arching story of whole cities, suburbs, or indeed neighbourhoods, and sought instead to understand the lives and life-cycles of individuals and groups with the city by using ethnographic sources to focus on smaller-scale aspects of urban and suburban culture. An emerging trend in Melbourne is for this to go further, and local histories now combine social and ethnographic history by taking the form of multi-authored volumes exploring different cultural and social aspects of neighbourhoods, especially in the inner city. Such collections have so far appeared on inner city Fitzroy, Brunswick and most recently, Carlton, but there is no reason why similar studies could not also be undertaken on the increasingly multicultural and socially diverse middle and outer suburbs.

This chapter attempts to tell Australia's urban story. It begins that task by setting out to interrogate the historical reasons for the suburban nature of Australian cities, before going on to challenge this 'suburban nation' thesis by drawing on my own work, which examines current political and social debates about the most appropriate built form of our cities from an historical perspective. This section demonstrates that alongside the suburban majority in Australia there has always existed a group who either sought or were forced by circumstance into more communal forms of living. The chapter then concludes by suggesting that these dwellings may be undergoing a revival in popularity as a result of new social, economic and cultural trends.

The idea of 'home'

To understand the power of the 'idea of home' is to understand Australia. Even the most casual observer of Australia's major cities and towns cannot fail to notice how low-slung and sprawling they are. But while studies of the 'exotic', and the cosmopolitan 'other', of the inner city have been popular topics of inquiry, until relatively recently few academic historians have been willing to venture into the history of the most characteristic habitat of Australians – the vast agglomerations of dormitory suburbs that are the dominant feature of Australian urban areas. In 1952 Robin Boyd, a young architect and scion of a great literary and artistic family, wrote that Australia is 'the small house'. What he meant was that Australia's cities, like those of the United States, Canada and other New World nations, are a physical testimony to the power of the attachment to 'home' and suburbia in Anglo-Saxon-derived cultures. The suburban ideal was, and to an extent remains, the social bedrock upon which Australian cities are based, as was the belief in the supremacy of the detached house over the flat, apartment or tenement.

As Graeme Davison has recently argued, 'Australia was born urban and quickly grew suburban', and 'from the outset, Australia's founders anticipated a sprawl of homes and gardens rather than a clumping of terraces and alleys'. The area of Australian cities – metropolitan Adelaide with a population of about 1.1 million is, at 1820 square kilometres, larger than Greater London with its population of 7 million – suggests that these early ideas have become a reality. Economic historian Lionel Frost has located the different Australian cities within a model of development he depicts as a 'New Urban Frontier' – the vast urban agglomerations of detached houses built in Australasia and the Pacific west coast of North America in the late nineteenth century. He suggests that low-density Melbourne, Adelaide and Perth fit this model very closely, while Sydney, Brisbane and Hobart, more densely populated, but still sprawling by world standards, are closer to an Atlantic or east coast United States model.[3] While Frost has credited the 'Great Australian Dream' of a detached, preferably owner-occupied house to comparatively good nineteenth-century wages and conditions, Graeme Davison has, accurately I think, seen the influence of 'more elusive, and largely non-quantifiable, social, cultural, and political factors' representative of the aspirations of citizens of an immigrant nation, mostly populated, at least initially, by settlers from England, Scotland and Ireland.

Australian cities should therefore be understood as physical manifestations of the cultural baggage of generations of immigrants, or in American historian Louis Hartz's evocative phrase, as 'fragments' of their parent societies, 'broken off' at a certain time and stage of

political and social development.[4] In the Australian case, Hartz's
fragment broke off not in one piece but at various times and places
over two centuries, and the shape of our cities provides evidence of
each of those fragments.[5] The first fragment was dumped at Sydney
in the late eighteenth century, which Hartz's colleague Richard Rosecrance recognised as representative of a strand of the lower levels of
British and Irish societies, victims of the twin pressures of the enclosure movement and the early stages of the Industrial Revolution.
Thus Sydney's earliest settlers were the poorest and most destitute
members of a rapidly changing society. They brought with them the
cultural baggage of a class that 'rejected the existing social order and
which began to seek political remedies for its difficulties'. Rosecrance
sees in these people the earliest adherents to a radical political position that eventually emerged as a form of what he calls Australia's
'"socialist" *laissez-faire*' political and economic system. They also
brought with them a desire for land and space.

    Like Davison, Sydney historian Grace Karskens has traced the
Australian attachment to the free-standing house to these earliest
years of the European occupation of Australia. Her study of Sydney's
Rocks, perhaps the first suburb in Australia, found that its spatial
form was a prototype for later urban development. Houses occupied
by 'artisans, small traders, shopkeepers and labourers, married and
unmarried couples', as well as less reputable members of the population and people associated with maritime activities, bore distinct similarities with those of the middle and upper classes 'across the water'
in Sydney proper. The houses were:

> set apart with a garden at the front bisected by a path … Those
> keen to assert a claim over the land they occupied fenced these
> gardens … The stout fences were also signs to others that the land
> had been appropriated not by deed, grant or lease but by de facto
> occupation.[6]

She goes on to argue that the urban form of the Rocks and Sydney
more generally was fashioned according to the 'tastes, priorities and

inclinations of the people'.

Why were these early Australians so keen on land and home-ownership and why did detached housing become so ubiquitous so quickly in Australia? Although Karskens does not provide an overt answer, it is most likely a result of an imported British distaste for urban life, and, more importantly, because among Sydney's earliest residents were also groups who saw Australia as a place of opportunity for material and social success denied them in Britain. Their desire for land and home-ownership was part of a desire for economic advancement. Rosecrance and others have argued that as well as the poor in the Rocks, there existed in early Sydney another group, 'the exclusives' – mostly ex-officers and free settlers – who were 'primarily interested in protecting [their] economic position', and establishing themselves as landholders and merchants. Graeme Davison has seen in this group the influence of the Evangelical Revival in England, and the social and cultural ideals of architect and landscape designer John Claudius Loudon. The exclusives and the earliest members of what was to become the colonial elite gravitated to the eastern shores of Sydney Harbour and built large country or suburban houses derived in part from the ideas that were then being popularised in England by Loudon and his associates. Their houses were statements of economic and social mobility and were most likely the model for the poor of the Rocks. They certainly became the basis for the spread of the suburban ideal throughout Australia, especially the belief that wealth could be achieved through real property accumulation.

Adelaide, Brisbane, Hobart, Melbourne and Perth were founded between fifteen and fifty years after Sydney and their early histories reflect events in Australia, Britain and Ireland in those intervening years. If Sydney was the prototype suburban city, Melbourne became the exemplar. As early as 1841, Melbourne's 'first suburb' Newtown (today's Fitzroy) was described as offering its inhabitants the opportunity to leave the pressures and unpleasantness of the central city for the charms and delights of residences 'dispersed throughout the many lovely spots with which it abounds'. Newtown's villas were described as 'romantic' and 'secluded', yet the suburb was 'near enough to Melbourne to be accessible for daily work'.[7] Urban historian Ian Turner has noted that by the early 1850s, this 'Newtown' style of living in detached houses had become the norm, or at least the desired norm, of Melbournians, who showed a remarkable preference for a semi-rural or suburban existence on 'the quarter or one-sixth acre block'.[8]

The various gold rushes of the early 1850s saw Australia's population almost treble in a decade. In what was by then the colony of Victoria, numbers had risen from under 100 000 in 1851 to over half a million ten years later. A new type of colonist had emerged in this much-expanded population – men and women who had been influenced by the Chartist movement in 1830s and 1840s Britain – and who brought with them some of the values of thrift, independence, and social and political rights associated with this philosophy. Rosecrance sees in this later fragment, the gold-rush generation, a group of 'independent seekers of fortune, animated by the desire to improve their condition and status', including their housing. They were not, however, proto-capitalists in the strict sense, because their desire for material advancement was 'tinctured with reformism' and the demands of the 'People's Charter' for manhood suffrage and some workers' rights. These were working-class ideals, but bore many similarities to traditionally bourgeois beliefs, especially in the importance of home-ownership.

Graeme Davison's *The Rise and Fall of Marvellous Melbourne*, a study of the city in the booming 1880s, suggests that the ideal of home-ownership and the benefits of suburban living became the mark of social respectability for both working and middle-class citizens in nineteenth-century Australia. By the early 1880s, about 45 per cent of all households in what was then Australia's largest city owned or were buying their own home. For the middle-class, suburbia and all it stood for became the model of lifestyle perfection. The suburban home was to be a retreat from the hustle and bustle of the business-oriented city and was 'the soul's defence against the metropolis, the social mechanism by which personal values, expunged from the work-a-day world, established their own domain'. It also became a way for the economically successful to assert their social and financial arrival. The grand towered mansion set in luxurious surrounds was the ultimate achievement but, as in Britain and America, the villa in a semi-rural suburb could be seen as the mansion or country house writ small, allowing the successful businessman to combine his need to be in the city near his workplace with the social and health benefits of a rural life.

The idea of home and the nuclear family were inextricably linked in an immigrant society, where extended intergenerational families were largely unknown. Suburbia was also predicated on the gendered division of labour, with the man of the house expected to go out to work in the 'bustling metropolis', while his wife tended to his needs in the 'haven' of repose that was the home. While feminist scholars in Australia and elsewhere have argued that the individual home is exploitative of women's labour and is symbolic of patriarchal capitalism's need for ever-larger markets for its products, the 'idea of home' appears to have been popular with the vast majority of Australians, women as well as men. It is perhaps because the suburbs have seemed so oppressive of women and because some aspired to a life beyond the domestic horizon, that they have traditionally had so few defenders among feminist and other progressive historians. This is now changing and scholars such as Jenny Gregory in Perth, Mark Peel in Adelaide and Grace Karskens in Sydney have attempted to reclaim the suburbs as places where men and women sought to build lives together, seeing their homes and families as signifiers of achievement, and markers of material triumph over the hardships and devastation of Depression and war.

In the post-war years the detached home in the suburbs became *the* symbol of Australian achievement. Both reformist Labor Party and conservative Liberal Party governments saw the detached, suburban home as the birthright of all Australians. Post-war Labor governments advocated some role for public provision, but essentially saw home-ownership as a worthy aspiration for their working-class constituency. Long-time conservative prime minister Robert Menzies was less enthusiastic about the role of the state. Rather, he saw a nation of home-owners as 'the foundation of sanity and sobriety' and the determinant of 'the health of society as a whole'. Like the Eisenhower Administration in the United States, his government pursued Fordist policies to ensure mass home-ownership and car-based cities. Through government control of the mortgage finance sector, low or no taxes on owner-occupied housing, and – in a pointer to later British policy – massive inducements for tenants to buy their publicly provided housing, Australia achieved one of the highest rates of home-ownership in the world – over 70 per cent at the end of the 'long boom' in the mid-1970s.

The detached owner-occupied house remains popular, and not just with Australians of British origin. Some of the highest rates of home-ownership are to be found amongst new immigrant groups – the wave after wave of new 'fragments' who have made Australia their home since 1945. But there are still critics who see Australia's suburbs as homogeneous, culturally barren places, insufferably dull and lethal to the human spirit. Comedian Barry Humphries has become internationally famous for his caricatures of Australian suburban ritual and lower middle-class respectability – Dame Edna Everage from Melbourne's Moonee Ponds chief among them. An emerging trend in Australian urban history, however, recognises that far from being homogeneous, Australia's suburbs are in fact amongst the most multicultural in the world. An increasing number of histories are appearing that chart the experiences of Indigenous people and non-English-speaking migrants and their families. Maria Nugent's work on La Perouse in Sydney, for instance, examines the survival and adaptive strategies of the local Indigenous population in one of the most historically contested parts of the city, a symbolic and literal place apart, with multiple meanings to Aboriginal and non-Aboriginal Australians. And migrants' stories of life in the suburbs are being told by their historian children and grandchildren. Thus Gioconda Di Lorenzo has produced accounts of poor Italian men and women working in and adapting to a new life in post-war suburban Melbourne, as has Tina Kalivas on the survival and modification of food cultures among Greek-Cypriot immigrants, also in Melbourne.

More compact cities?

While some historians are now celebrating the suburbs, other important groups continue to denounce them. In recent years a debate has emerged about whether the detached suburban house is still affordable in economic, social and environmental terms. A new group of influential critics now portray the 'great Australian dream' as responsible for high infrastructure and land costs, social anomie and the unsustainable use of non-renewable energy sources. These battles are largely being waged by architects, planners and social scientists, many of whom seem to have little if any knowledge of the historical forces that shaped Australia's cities. My recent book *Together Apart* looks at the history of communal forms of living.[9] It challenges both traditional assumptions about the extent and primacy of the 'idea of the home' and the ahistorical nature of the current debates about New Urbanism and what is usually called 'urban consolidation' in Australia. Focusing on pre-war Melbourne, I have used a range of ethnographic sources to argue that, alongside the detached family home, there has long existed an array of dwelling options including boarding houses, tenements, hostels and flats available for those unable or unwilling to adopt the suburban ideal. I also suggest that a return to providing a range of communal dwelling options, that combine private bathing and other amenities with semi-public gathering spaces, might be a way for our cities to develop in the twenty-first century.

In the nineteenth and early twentieth century, boarding houses provided accommodation for single men and women who chose or were forced to live outside the traditional nuclear family. But these places bore little resemblance to the sort of accommodation-of-last-resort associated with the type today. Many were quite luxurious and well appointed, and were the preferred residence of many well-to-do citizens, especially single and widowed women. There was, however, a clear difference between 'boarding' and 'lodging' houses - an important distinction which has usually been lost in studies of this sector in Australia. A lodging house essentially provided low-cost nightly accommodation to the poor and the transient, while a boarding house was a place where tenants were sheltered for more than a week at a time and were provided with meals as part of the tariff. My focus is on what were known as 'first class' or 'high class' boarding or 'guest' houses, the existence of which illuminates the changing nature of accommodation offered to non-traditional, but still essentially middle- to upper-class, householders. Before the inter-war years there were strict legal and social differences between boarding and lodging, but my work demonstrates that a gradual blurring of these boundaries meant that both became subject to intense scrutiny and control.

As the social status of the boarding house declined in the first decades of the twentieth century, a series of mostly church-based hostels were developed around the fringes of city centres to cater for a new urban dweller – the city 'business girl'. As with the North American experience, these hostels were a reaction to fears expressed by religious and other commentators about the opportunities and perceived dangers which cities held for the relatively large numbers of young women coming to the city to work in the new 'pink collar' and manufacturing jobs. The hostels were designed as safe and 'respectable' refuges for young women deemed too naive to understand the potentially dangerous ways of the city. They had a protective function, but for many young women they were also an important stepping stone into the ways and opportunities of the cities, providing shelter, but also access to a wide group of people – mostly in their teens and twenties, and of a similar religion and social class – with all that meant for a social life in the city. Residents formed life-long friendships and also met potential partners among the brothers and friends of other hostel dwellers.

Flats (apartments) also came to Australian cities in the early twentieth century. Sydney saw the greatest growth in these types of dwellings, mainly around the harbour and ocean beaches. In Melbourne they were mostly built in the inner eastern and southern suburbs. Few flats were built in the other cities until the 1960s, largely because demand for land and dwellings was not so strong elsewhere – although Jenny Gregory and Robin Taylor have shown that there was some flat development in Perth in the inter-war years. The coming of flats to Australia was seen in some quarters as a disturbing example of the loosening of traditional social and living patterns, and flats and flat-dwellers were subject to scrutiny and denunciation by upholders of Anglo-Saxon values. Flats were portrayed as alien to Australian traditions, destroyers of families and home life, and likely to undermine home ownership and individual effort. 'It tears down character so, this flat and hotel life', wrote Sydney architectural commentator Florence Taylor in 1909. 'A woman grows self-centred and fretful because she has nothing to do', while 'a girl becomes selfish and blasé because she thinks only of her pleasures, and because she sees those about her thinking of only themselves and their pleasures'.[10]

The building of flats and the lifestyles of their tenants were a frequently discussed topic in social and architectural circles in the inter-war years, and featured in many stories in the daily papers and popular magazines, especially in the mid-to-late 1930s. Many of these commentators saw the arrival of flats as a breath of fresh air and European sophistication into what they saw as Australia's stifling Anglo-Saxon culture. Writing in the *Journal of the Royal Victorian Institute of Architects* in 1938, architect Robert Hamilton derided Melbourne's aversion to the flat as evidence of a 'people influenced by facile transport arrangements and climatic conditions [to] either the individual house or the smaller type of flat building'. He compared Melbourne with Sydney, where, he said, 'the sense for living in flats' had developed 'to a much stronger degree'. Even so, Australian cities in general were far behind 'leading cities abroad', especially in Europe where building regulations allowed for a far greater number of flats to be built, and where 'the general desire of the people [is] to reside near the heart of the city'.

For many Australians, boarding, lodging and flat-dwelling have represented unpleasant reminders of Old World communality and renting rather than owner-occupation, and as such have been deemed an, at best, second-rate housing solution. As we have seen, advocates of 'Australian values' denounced the notion of communal living, and saw these places as scourges best resisted if national life and character were to prosper. My work on these places therefore has similarities with studies of British and North American experiences of communal living documented by Richard Harris, Paul Groth, Richard Dennis and others. There is a growing literature on boarding, lodging and hostel-dwelling in these countries, although, as with the Australian experience, there is often a conflation in this literature between the formal and the informal sectors of the boarding and lodging market. Similarly, the rise of the urban flat in these countries has been increasingly documented over the last decade or so. The demand for flats and supervised and unsupervised boarding-house accommodation in these countries similarly came from the growing number of non-nuclear family households, and also caused anxiety for the many who remained attached to traditional ideas about appropriate housing and domestic life. This widespread demand also suggests these dwellings represented one outcome of the mobilisation and dislocation unleashed by the rise of Modernism and new methods of production reshaping Western societies from the middle of the nineteenth century. Such demand is, lastly, also representative of changes in gender roles in the twentieth century, especially in the inter-war period.

More work needs to be done on the history of all of these accommodation types and their residents in Australia, if for no better reason than to inform current-day policy-makers about the potential for a variety of dwelling types in the twenty-first century. To the student of the early twentieth-century debates, current discussions about changing demographics and the rise of an urban culture in Australia's cities have an uncanny resemblance to the more optimistic urbanists of half a century or more ago. So too do the sometimes shrill responses of residents and residents' action groups to the arrival of multi-unit dwellings into traditional suburban streetscapes. What these recurring debates suggest is that not only are important sections of the urban policy-making class in Australia ignorant of current debates in urban history, but also that there exists an unfortunate tendency to see the urban past in overtly didactic terms of 'urban' versus 'suburban' values. My work shows that the reality is much more complex and that a minority urban tradition has long existed beside the suburban majority. There is no reason why this cannot continue into the twenty-first century.

The re-emergence of a debate about the most appropriate dwelling forms for Australians in the twenty-first century demonstrates that the earliest Australian urban historians were right when they argued that cities and urban areas are a function of economic, social and demographic change. The current rapid increase in demand for inner-urban dwellings is evidence that just as in the nineteenth and twentieth centuries, when Australian cities developed distinctive forms in response to pressures of and resistance to changing global economic structures, so too are our present-day cities and city-dwellers dealing with powerful historical forces, in this case post-industrial global capitalism. This is especially noticeable in Sydney, the Australian city most completely enmeshed in the global finance industry. Since the 1960s, Australia's inner cities have also been transformed by gentrification, and the displacement of the poor, the immigrant and unskilled, by tertiary-educated 'knowledge workers'. Whereas the inner city was historically associated with poverty, vice and 'foreign-ness', today the emphasis is on consumption, 'lifestyle' and cosmopolitanism. Similar pressures on property prices, tenure and dwelling options are being felt in most major world cities, as has recently been documented by a range of geographers, sociologists and urban economists. These changes in urban structures and the rapid transformations of cities in response to changing economic and social patterns, however, await detailed scrutiny by historians in Australia and elsewhere.

But, as with the other changes in the dwelling structures of our cities documented in this chapter, these contemporary pressures need to be viewed from cultural as well as economic perspectives. Demands for a broader range of dwelling-types in Australia are reflective of new and emerging shelter requirements of an aging population and of people whose cultural influences are not of Anglo-Saxon derivation. These demands also come in part from an increase in the number of single-female households. As in the inter-war years, many women are today taking advantage of changed economic and social patterns to pursue lifestyle and career options that were until recently denied them. Many see an inner-city apartment as the most appropriate and secure solution to their housing needs, although whether they will seek more traditional suburban dwellings when and if they choose to have children remains to be seen. Ultimately perhaps, what these ongoing debates about how Australians should live really mean is that two generations of urban historians were right about the primacy of the city, and that in order to better understand Australia's past and potentially its future, we first need to know about and attempt to understand its cities, suburbs and people.

Notes

1   G Davison, 'Australia: the first suburban nation?', *Journal of Urban History*, 22:1, November 1995, pp 40-74.
2   G Davison, *The Rise and Fall of Marvellous Melbourne*, Melbourne, 1978.
3   L Frost, *The New Urban Frontier: urbanisation and city-building in Australasia and the American West*, Sydney, 1991.
4   L Hartz (ed), *The Founding of New Societies: studies in the history of the United States, Latin America, South Africa, Canada, and Australia*, New York, 1964.
5   R Rosecrance, 'The radical culture of Australia', in L Hartz, *Founding of New Societies*, pp 275-318.
6   G Karskens, 'The dialogue of townscape: The Rocks and Sydney 1788–1820',

Australian Historical Studies, 108, 1997, pp 88-112; see also her larger study, *The Rocks: everyday life in early Sydney*, Melbourne, 1997, esp ch 4, 'Patterns of occupation'.

7   RD Murray, *A Summer at Port Phillip*, quoted in J Grant and G Serle (eds) *The Melbourne Scene 1803–1956*, Melbourne, 1956, pp 38–39.

8   I Turner, 'The growth of Melbourne' in JW McCarty and CB Schedvin (eds), *Australian Capital Cities: historical essays*, Sydney, 1978, p 73

9   S O'Hanlon, *Together Apart: boarding-house, hostel and flat life in pre-war Melbourne*, Melbourne, 2002.

10   *Building*, 8 April 1909.

FURTHER READING

Many signposts for further reading are given in the notes for each chapter and in the Notes on Contributors, and so this section is intended only to direct the reader towards some general introductory histories, and a few notable works.

David Day's *Claiming a Continent* (Sydney, 1996) is a readable general introduction, but is currently out of print. Other introductions are provided by Stuart Macintyre, *A Concise History of Australia* (rev edn, Melbourne, 2004), and the classic but idiosyncratic *Short History of Australia* (Melbourne, 1995) by CMH (Manning) Clark, which is a distillation of his six-volume *A History of Australia* (Melbourne, 1962–1987). For more recent scholarly treatment, consult the *Oxford History of Australia*, (Melbourne, 1988-1996), with individual volumes written by Jan Kociumbas, Beverley Kingston, Stuart Macintyre and Geoffrey Bolton, who is also the general editor of the series. *A People's History of Australia since 1788*, edited by Verity Burgmann and Jenny Lee (Melbourne, 1988) is an interesting but uneven collection which self-consciously explores Australian history from below. A recent popular social history is Geoffrey Blainey, *Black Kettle and Full Moon* (Camberwell, 2003).

On the history wars, readers should consider the embattled Keith Windschuttle's *The Fabrication of Aboriginal history* (Sydney, 2002). Windschuttle's targets include Lyndall Ryan, *The Aboriginal Tasmanians* (Sydney, 1996) and Henry Reynolds who, in a series of books including *The Other Side of the Frontier* (Melbourne, 1981), has presented a nuanced picture of both white/Aboriginal conflict and co-operation. The debates are discussed in Stuart Macintyre and Anna Clark, *The History Wars* (Melbourne, 2003), and (somewhat polemically) in Robert Manne's edition, *Whitewash* (Melbourne, 2003). Most recently, the history wars have sparked a series of historians' reflections on their craft in Stuart Macintyre's edition, *The Historian's Conscience* (Melbourne, 2004). Important contributions to the history of white/Aboriginal relations are also provided by Inga Clendinnen,

Dancing With Strangers (Melbourne, 2003), Heather Goodall, *Invasion to Embassy: land in Aboriginal politics in New South Wales 1770-1972* (Sydney, 1996), and Russell McGregor, *Imagined Destinies: Aboriginal Australians and the doomed race theory 1880-1939* (Melbourne, 1997). On the 'stolen generations' issue, see Anna Haebich, *Broken Circles: fragmenting Indigenous families 1800-2000* (Fremantle, 2000).

On urban history, see the important contribution of Graeme Davison, *The Rise and Fall of Marvellous Melbourne* (Melbourne, 1978), which combines economic and social history in accounting for Melbourne's spectacular growth in the 1880s. Peter Spearritt, *Sydney's Century: a history* (Sydney, 1999) begins with the rise of suburbia and ends with the post-industrial metropolis of the 2000 Olympics. See also Mark Peel, *The Lowest Rung: voices of Australian poverty* (Melbourne, 2003), and Seamus O'Hanlon, *Together Apart: boarding house, hostel and flat life in pre-war Melbourne* (Melbourne, 2002).

Australian historians have made a significant contribution to the history of the Great War and modern memory. Consult Ken Inglis, *Sacred Places: war memorials in the Australian landscape* (Melbourne, 1998), and the oral historian Alistair Thomson's *Anzac Memories: living with the legend* (Melbourne, 1994).

In the rich vein of Australian cultural history, see John Rickard, *Australia: a cultural history* (London, 1988 and 2000), and Russel Ward's now classic statement of the mythology of the bush, *The Australian Legend* (Melbourne, 1958). The collection by Hsu-Ming Teo and Richard White, *Cultural History in Australia* (Sydney, 2003) is a lively introduction to the varieties of cultural history methods pursued by Australian historians. Fundamental aspects of Australian society and culture are treated in two volumes by Alan Atkinson, *The Europeans in Australia: a history* (Melbourne 1997 & 2004), Penny Russell, *A Wish of Distinction: colonial gentility and femininity* (Melbourne, 1994), and Richard Waterhouse *Private Pleasures, Public Leisure* (Melbourne, 1995). Questions of national identity recur, for example in Richard White, *Inventing Australia: images and identity 1688-1980* (Sydney, 1981) and Patricia Grimshaw et al, *Creating a Nation* (Melbourne, 1994). The colonists' imaginative engagement with their new environment is explored in such studies as Tim Bonyhady, *The Colonial Earth* (Melbourne, 2000) and Tom Griffiths, *Hunters and Collectors: the antiquarian imagination in Australia* (Cambridge, 1996).

Traditions of Australian democracy and radicalism are dissected by John Hirst, *Strange Birth of Colonial Democracy: New South Wales 1848-1884* (Sydney, 1988), Bruce Scates, *A New Australia: citizenship, radicalism and the First Republic* (Melbourne, 1997) and Mark McKenna, *The Captive Republic* (Melbourne, 1996).

Among the most influential feminist scholarship are Marilyn Lake, *Getting Equal: the history of Australian feminism* (Sydney, 1999), and Susan Magarey et al's collection, *Debutante Nation: feminism contests the 1890s* (Sydney, 1993). Convict women have been well covered by the demographic historian Deborah Oxley, *Convict Maids: the forced migration of women to Australia* (Melbourne, 1996) and by Joy Damousi, *Depraved and Disorderly: female convicts, sexuality and gender in colonial Australia* (Cambridge, 1997).

On relations with Asia, see Sean Brawley, *The White Peril: foreign relations and Asian immigration to Australasia and North America 1919-78* (Sydney, 1995) and the highly readable David Walker, *Anxious Nation: Australia and the rise of Asia 1850-1939* (Brisbane, 1999).

INDEX

Also published by UNSW Press

ANCIENT AND MODERN
Time, Culture and Indigenous Philosophy

Stephen Muecke

How might we think and talk about indigenous philosophy? Why has Aboriginal knowledge not been given the status of philosophical knowledge, but treated by whites rather as culture or history?

This is the starting point for the essays contained in Stephen Muecke's original and challenging book. Blending anecdote, theory and personal reflection, Muecke moves from film to travel to politics to religion, gathering knowledge, revisiting theory and recasting key assumptions.

With passion and conviction, and a sense of experiment and discovery, *Ancient & Modern* calls for a new kind of modernity.

STEPHEN MUECKE holds a Personal Chair in Cultural Studies at the University of Technology, Sydney, and is a Fellow of the Australian Academy of the Humanities. His books include (with Paddy Roe and Krim Benterrak): *Reading the Country: Introduction to Nomadology* (1984, 1996); *Textual Spaces: Aboriginality and Cultural Studies* (1992); the fictocritical *No Road (bitumen all the way)*; a translation of José Gil's *Metamorphoses of the Body* (1998); and the children's story *About this little devil and this little fella*, edited for Albert Barunga (1999). He recently edited (with Adam Shoemaker) David *Unaipon's Legendary Tales of the Australian Aborigines* (2001). He is co-editor of *The Cultural Studies Review*.

ISBN 0 86840 786 0

Also published by UNSW Press

FREUD IN THE ANTIPODES:
A cultural history of psychoanalysis in Australia

Joy Damousi

Psychoanalysis – one of the most important intellectual developments of the twentieth century – is perhaps as much a cultural experience as a clinical one. This groundbreaking book is the first to examine the history and impact of Freudian ideas in Australia. Joy Damousi shows that ways of understanding our emotional and interior lives have a notable and complex history that challenges Australian stereotypes of shallow hedonism and emotional barrenness. By linking psychoanalysis with modernity, the book is, in effect, an alternative history of twentieth-century Australia.

'This is a brilliant book. Without replicating the research or conclusions of any existing work, the author has produced . . . a work that will be eagerly read by scholars of Australian intellectual history, the history of psychoanalysis and the human sciences, and the intersection of science and popular culture.'

– Dr Richard C. Keller, Dept. of Medical History and Bioethics, University of Wisconsin-Madison

JOY DAMOUSI is the author of several books including: *Depraved and Disorderly: Female Convicts, Sexuality and Gender in Colonial Australia* (1997); *Living With the Aftermath: Trauma, Nostalgia and Grief in Post-War Australia* (2001); with Robert Reynolds (eds) *Psychoanalysis, History and Identities, Melbourne* (2003).

ISBN   0 86840 888 3

Also published by UNSW Press

GOD'S WILLING WORKERS
Women and Religion in Australia

Anne O'Brien

God's Willing Workers examines the ways religious beliefs and institutions shaped the lives of women in Australia over 200 years. Dealing with both Catholic and Protestant traditions it analyses the various ways nuns, missionaries and women in domestic settings interpreted church teachings and examines the huge impact of mid-20th century feminism on women in their relationship with the church.

At the heart of Anne O'Brien's discussion is a drive to understand the diverse religious experiences of Australian women during the past two centuries. *God's Willing Workers* explores the role that gender has played in shaping these experiences and, in doing so, unveils some of the unique ways in which women have responded to religious teachings and institutions. Ultimately, this is a book about hope and disappointment, about generosity and its limits.

ANNE O'BRIEN graduated from the University of Adelaide with an Honours degree in history and took a PhD from the University of Sydney. The author of *Poverty's Prison: The poor in NSW 1880–1918* she has worked as a secondary school teacher, project officer with the Bicentennial Local History Coordination Project and now teaches in the School of History at the University of New South Wales.

ISBN   0 86840 575 2

Also published by UNSW Press

IS HISTORY FICTION?

Anne Curthoys and John Docker

How can we in the present know the past? Is history a science? Can history have general laws? What was the linguistic turn? What has happened in the new millennium to the experimental thinking and literary innovation of the 1980s and 1990s? Does the Holocaust show how wrong postmodernism is? Why have History Wars occurred in so many parts of the world in the last two decades?

ANN CURTHOYS is a well-known historian and public intellectual. Her fields of expertise include: indigenous and migration history, feminist theory and the history of feminism, history of the media and popular culture, history of genocide in relation to settler colonialism, theories of history. She was GO8 Visiting Professor in Australian studies at Georgetown University, Washington DC, in 2003-04. Her most recent book, *Freedom Ride: A Freedomrider Remembers* won the 2003 Stanner Award.

JOHN DOCKER is a well-known literary and cultural critic, and public intellectual. He has written on Australian literary and cultural history; contemporary theories of culture, identity, colonialism, and diaspora; Orientalism and exoticism; monotheism and polytheism; and genocide in relation both to the Enlightenment and colonialism. His many books include *Postmodernism and Popular Culture: A Cultural History* (also translated into Chinese) and most recently *1492: The Poetics of Diaspora*.

ISBN 0 86840 734 8

Also published by UNSW Press

LOOKING FOR BLACKFELLAS' POINT

Mark McKenna

Winner of:
- *Book of the Year NSW Premier's Literary Awards 2003*
- *Douglas Stewart Non-Fiction Prize NSW Premier's Awards 2003*
- *Australian Cultural Studies Award 2002*

Blackfellas' Point, once an Aboriginal camping ground and meeting place on the Towamba river in south-eastern New South Wales, is the starting point for this poignant exploration of Australian cultural identity and history. From the familiar vantage point of Blackfellas' Point McKenna unravels his history of Australian identity: a history that resonates with a sense of place.

Through intimate, descriptive prose McKenna unveils the politics of injustice and oppression intrinsic to our cultural history and identity. In doing so he expresses the desire of both Indigenous and non-Indigenous Australians to reconcile this history through political and social change in the 20th century and beyond.

'A powerful meditation, in local and national terms, on the continuing meaning of dispossession . . . McKenna's book burns with a fierce and loving commitment to the place, its history and all its people.'
– Peter Read, *The Age*

'McKenna's ambition is . . . amply fulfilled. To hear the silences, to see the absences, to be hopeful in awful circumstances takes a special sort of sensitivity. McKenna tells his true stories with gentle grace.'
– Greg Dening, *The London Review of Books*

ISBN 0 86840 644 9

Also published by UNSW Press

REPORTS FROM A WILD COUNTRY
Ethics for Decolonisation

Deborah Bird Rose

Captain Cook was the real wild one. He failed to recognise Law, destroyed people and country, lived by damage and promoted cruelty.

Reports from a Wild Country explores some of Australia's major ethical challenges. Written in the midst of rapid social and environmental change and in a time of uncertainty and division, it offers powerful stories and arguments for ethical choice and commitment. The focus is on reconciliation between Indigenous and 'Settler' peoples, and with nature.

With a distinctive and powerful voice, Deborah Bird Rose draws on case studies from across Australia to show pathways toward decolonisation, and indicts a few that continue to perpetrate violence. Based on a pronounced moral engagement between past and present, the book affirms the power of ethics, resilence and love in these difficult and demanding times.

DEBORAH BIRD ROSE is a senior research scholar and prize-winning author. An anthropologist by training, she has worked with Aboriginal people in their claims to land, in protecting sacred sites and in collaboratively documenting their relationships with totemic landscapes. Her previous books include *Country of the Heart: An Indigenous Australian Homeland*, *Dingo Makes Us Human: Life and Land in an Australian Aboriginal Culture* and *Hidden Histories: Black Stories from Victoria River Downs, Humbert River and Wave Hill Stations*.

ISBN 0 86840 798 4

Also published by UNSW Press

WESTMINSTER LEGACIES
Democracy and Responsible Government in Asia and
the Pacific

Edited by Haig Patapan,
John Wanna and Patrick Weller

Westminster Legacies examines the ways in which the Westminster system has been influential in shaping responsible government and democracy across Asia, Australasia and the Pacific. It devotes chapters to each of the following countries: India, Pakistan, Nepal, Singapore, Malaysia, Australia, New Zealand, Papua New Guinea, Fiji and the smaller Pacific island nations.

Westminster Legacies explores the way Westminster understandings of the executive, bureaucracy, parliament and responsible government have been influential in these countries – home to such diverse histories, cultures and traditions. It examines the ways the Westminster system has been adapted in the light of local practices and traditions, and considers how Westminster remains important for understanding political institutions and practices in these countries.

It also looks at the conditions under which Westminster legacies have taken root and endured, and those conditions that have eroded or significantly changed its influence. Some of the countries *Westminster Legacies* surveys have teetered on the edge of becoming 'failed states' (especially in terms of legitimate democracies), while others remain robust adversarial democracies.

ISBN 0 86840 848 4